RURAL STUDIO

RURAL STUDIO

Samuel Mockbee and an Architecture of Decency

text by **ANDREA OPPENHEIMER DEAN**

photographs by **TIMOTHY HURSLEY**

and essays by **LAWRENCE CHUA** *and* **CERVIN ROBINSON**

PRINCETON ARCHITECTURAL PRESS   NEW YORK

PUBLISHED BY

Princeton Architectural Press

37 East Seventh Street

New York, New York 10003

For a free catalog of books, call 1.800.722.6657.
Visit our web site at www.papress.com.

EDITING: Clare Jacobson
DESIGN: Sara E. Stemen

SPECIAL THANKS TO: Nettie Aljian, Ann Alter,
Amanda Atkins, Nicola Bednarek, Janet Behning,
Megan Carey, Penny Chu, Jan Cigliano, Jane Garvie,
Tom Hutten, Mark Lamster, Nancy Eklund Later,
Linda Lee, Anne Nitschke, Evan Schoninger,
Lottchen Shivers, Jennifer Thompson, and Deb Wood
of Princeton Architectural Press
—Kevin C. Lippert, publisher

LIBRARY OF CONGRESS CATALOGING-IN-PUBLICATION DATA

Dean, Andrea Oppenheimer.

   Rural Studio : Samuel Mockbee and an architecture of decency / text by Andrea Oppenheimer Dean
and photographs by Timothy Hursley ; with essays by
Lawrence Chua and Cervin Robinson.

   p.   cm.

Includes bibliographical references.

   ISBN 1-56898-292-5 (alk. paper)

   1. Auburn University. Dept. of Architecture. Rural
Studio. 2. Architecture—Study and teaching—
Alabama—Hale County. 3. Vernacular architecture—
Alabama—Hale County. 4. Sustainable architecture—
Alabama—Hale County. 5. Poor—Housing—
Alabama—Hale County. 6. Mockbee, Samuel.
I. Hursley, Timothy, 1955– II. Auburn University.
School of Architecture. III. Title.

   NA2300.A9 D43 2002

   720'.71'176143—dc21

                                        2001003805

NOTE FROM THE AUTHORS

To our sorrow, Samuel Mockbee died of complications
of leukemia on December 30, 2001. We miss him.

CONTENTS

Shepard Bryant, a Rural Studio client, and his grandsons and their catch from the Black Warrior River

INTRODUCTION

IN HALE COUNTY, ALABAMA, you see ghost buildings: abandoned barns, tumbledown shanties, and rusted trailers—fragile remnants of a more prosperous agrarian past. You see old people sitting quietly on sagging porches and scruffy chicken hens noisily pecking and wandering on hard dirt yards. Hale is a left-behind place. But it is also a land of dense piney woods, fragrant crop furrows, and hypnotic rolling hills. It is the land of the Black Warrior River, "drifting among the dreams of the neglected . . . his ancient liquid light flowing toward (you and) the unknown," as an architect named Samuel Mockbee wrote in a poetic moment. In Hale County Mockbee found "an almost supernatural beauty," and mainly for that reason he decided to locate his Rural Studio there. He was familiar with Walker Evans and James Agee's Depression-era descriptions of impoverished sharecroppers in *Let Us Now Praise Famous Men*, which brought Hale County to national attention. But it did not figure into Mockbee's decision. Hale County seduced him, pure and simple.

When Mockbee founded the Rural Studio in the early 1990s, American architecture had retreated from social and civic engagement to a preoccupation with matters of style. The architectural stars, swept up in the new global economy and entranced by new technologies, were designing increasingly audacious buildings for affluent clients worldwide. Mockbee instead was digging in at home in the Deep South, focusing on the design and construction of modest, innovative houses for poor people. When he first set out in 1992 with twelve Auburn University architecture students in tow, Mockbee thought he was embarking on a one-year educational experiment. Nearly a decade later, the fifty-seven-year-old designer still leaves his home in Canton, Mississippi, most Monday mornings, drives 170 miles due east into Newbern, Alabama, a one-store hamlet that has become the Rural Studio's base, and spends the rest of the week working and living with students in a rundown 1890s farmhouse. The activity, he says, is "24-7. If you're going to do this you gotta pack your bags, kiss your wife goodbye, and go to war." Strong words from the least belligerent and dogmatic of men.

Naive as it may sound, Mockbee, a MacArthur "genius grant" recipient in 2000, is battling for convictions. One is that the architectural profession has an ethical responsibility to help improve living conditions for the poor. Another is that the profession should "challenge the status quo into making responsible environmental and social changes." Hence his belief that architectural education should expand its curriculum from "paper architecture" to the creation of real buildings and to sowing "a moral sense of service to the community." Architecture

1

students are typically middle-class youngsters working on theoretical designs. But those at Auburn University's Rural Studio are engaged in hands-on design and construction and in nose-to-nose negotiations with impoverished clients. You will find Mockbee there bucking his profession's prevailing emphasis on fashion, frantic speed, and superstardom to devote himself to the patient work of getting inexpensive but striking structures shaped and built by students while teaching them the fundamentals, not only of design and construction, but also of decency and fairness. How old-fashioned and refreshing!

Hale County lies just southwest of the industrial area surrounding Birmingham, and most of it is in the Black Belt, named for the dark, rich loam amid mustard- to rust-colored earth covering a crescent of central Alabama and northern Mississippi. The red soil that coats Hale County's hills and farmlands was stained by the same iron-rich clay that once fired Birmingham's steel mills. In the nineteenth century, the county retreated from slavery-based plantations and became a place left poor by Confederate defeat. The last century brought new scourges: soil erosion, the boll weevil, the collapse of the cotton market, and massive out-migration. Farmers who remained converted their land for cattle and soybeans, and most failed again. The newest "crop," catfish, thrives in still ponds occasionally visible from the road. But Hale County, with a poverty rate of nearly forty percent, still looks eerily similar to Evans and Agee's 1930s picture of it.

Slowly, the Rural Studio is inscribing its mark on Hale County. Into the community of Mason's Bend and the towns of Newbern, Sawyerville, Greensboro, Thomaston, and Akron, the studio has inserted simple but inventive structures made of inexpensive, mostly salvaged or donated, often curious materials—beat-up railroad ties, old bricks, donated lumber, hay bales, baled corrugated cardboard, rubber tires

Mockbee and students at president's mansion of Old Southern University

worn thin, license plates, and road signs. The studio's esthetic vocabulary is modern, but its buildings, with their protective roofs and roomy porches, shedlike forms and quirky improvisations, look right at home here. In Mockbee's view, "The best way to make real architecture is by letting a building evolve out of the culture and place. These small projects designed by students at the studio remind us what it means to have an American architecture without pretense. They offer us a simple glimpse into what is essential to the future of American architecture, its honesty."

The Rural Studio students are familiar to people in Hale and apparently well received. "At least about eighty percent of the time, we're welcome," says Craig Peavy, a fifth-year studio student in 2000/01. From living quarters in Newbern, Akron, and Hale's county seat of

Greensboro, students fan out each day to work on construction sites, attend city council meetings, confer with the county Department of Human Resources (which provides lists of needy clients from which students make selections), meet with the nonprofit HERO (Hale Empowerment and Revitalization Organization), and attend community catfish fries. For many students, this "classroom of the community," as Mockbee calls it, is the first intimate experience with "the smell and feel of poverty." Bruce Lanier, who graduated in 2000 and then went to work with a statewide rural poverty agency in Alabama, recalls, "I'd only driven through that kind of poverty on my way to private school. At the studio I learned that economic poverty is not a poverty of values but a fact of birth. You come to realize it's the luck of the draw that you don't end up poor. You learn poor people are like you and me. You get to know them and respect them." The experience of Lanier and others seems to confirm Mockbee's hope that exposing students to poverty, rather than preaching to them about it, can replace misconceptions fed by detachment with a willingness to understand and empathize with the down-and-out.

Architects have long criticized their profession's defining educational experience, the studio, where students, working under an established architect, are given a design problem, come up with a solution, flesh it out with floor plans and elevations, and defend it in a public session called a crit. Josh Cooper, a 1997 Auburn graduate, recalls that what he learned in class did not make sense until he began working on the Bryant House in Mason's Bend as a second-year student at the Rural Studio. "Rather than drawing a window and not having a clue what I was drawing," he says, "there was now a client standing there, and that window had to work for him. On a different level, I gained a lot of confidence knowing I could make that window work."

The studio offers a fifteen-hour course of study for second- and fifth-year students, equivalent in content to what their classmates take 150 miles away at Auburn. Each semester, fifteen second-year students help design and build a house and learn social and ethical responsibilities associated with architecture. They also receive instruction in materials and methods and in architectural history, which takes students to nearby farms and antebellum houses. About fifteen fifth-year students, meanwhile, stay at the studio an entire academic year, designing and building a community project and doing "neckdown" work, as Professor Andrew Freear characterizes required volunteer duty.

The students learn to work as a team. "We are taught in architectural education to be tortured artists," says Freear. "The fact is, architecture is teamwork, and this is the first time most students have worked with someone else." Jen Stanton, a second-year student in 2000, explains, "We do everything as a group and learn to compromise. Sometimes we yell at each other, but we learn to figure things out together."

Mockbee presents architecture as a discipline rooted in community and its environmental, social, political, and esthetic issues and shows students that they can make a difference. He tells them that as architects their goodness is more important than their greatness, their compassion more eventful than their passion.

It is evident to students, to the studio's two teachers (Freear and Steve Hoffman), and to its clients that Sambo, as everyone calls Mockbee, is the mind and soul of the Rural Studio. A bearded, bearish, fifth-generation Mississippian, he tools around Hale County in an old truck, and he usually wears baggy sweatpants, worn sneakers, and an Auburn baseball cap. He seems to be known to everyone in the county, presenting himself, in Lanier's words, as "a cross between a

Mississippi redneck and an art freak." Students pick up on his humane qualities and his moral sense. Andy Olds, a fifth-year student in 2000/01, says he envies his teacher's "humility as much as his success." Freear respects the fact that "Sambo works his heart out"; Hoffman that "Sambo's got the magic. He knows how to work with people." Hoffman mentions his lack of dogmatism and boldness that teaches students "to dive in." Stanton says, "Sambo doesn't tower over us; he's real comforting. He's an honest, good guy." Of himself Mockbee says, in the deep drawl of his region, "Don't overdo my unselfishness. I think saints are really self-serving. Not that I'm a saint." He jests about "a Santa Claus complex, just wanting everyone to be happy," saying, "What I do is self-serving, because I get to use my natural talents and sensibilities, education and imagination."

In bringing the studio to where it is today, Mockbee has honed an unusual combination of talents. Observe him in his workroom at the studio: He is on the telephone negotiating with a local merchant about insulation. He hangs up and tells his students, "Okay, I'll order some and let y'all experiment with it." Back on the phone, he banters with one of the many benefactors who supplied the studio with more than $2 million in grants and contributions between 1993 and 2000. (Auburn pays only Mockbee's, Freear's, and Hoffman's salaries.) Another call, and he finalizes plans for a lecture at the University of Arkansas; later he talks with a television producer coming to film the studio and then discusses a building repair with one of three inmates who are at the studio on work-release from the State Cattle Ranch. "They're pretty good teachers," he says. "Most students have never been around inmates before. Seeing they're just human takes out the abstraction."

If you ask Mockbee about founding the Rural Studio, he will tell you it was a "collaging of different experiences I had over the years, thinking all the time how I could push architecture, social improvement, education, arts and ideas about the environment." He will also tell you that he is "always trying to put together wonderful projects, large and small. Sometimes I'll see an opportunity that's only partially in place, and I'll sit on it until something else comes along that I can dovetail it with."

To find the pieces that came together to form the Rural Studio, Mockbee started with his family. "My mother was sweet and smart and educated, morally and ethically, the daughter of a Baptist minister; her family were educators." Mockbee's paternal grandmother, Sweet Tee, was the family's main financial support and a powerful influence on her grandson. In addition to having a strong personality, he says, she was outgoing, "very loving, loyal to her friends, a good businesswoman. I would say I'm somewhat similar in disposition." He describes his father, who trained to be a dentist and became a funeral home director, as "a typical southern man, hunting, fishing, gambling, and drinking." His drinking, however, turned to alcoholism, and, by the time Mockbee was twelve, his father had contracted tuberculosis. "From about his early forties he didn't work; he just stayed upstairs and drank and fed his squirrels and birds out the window. He was a sweet guy, a sweet alcoholic. I only resented that it was hard on my Mother." Mockbee's father died of cancer, the family curse. The disease claimed his mother and his only sibling, Martha Anne, who gave him the nickname "Sambo" and in 1998, after he learned he had leukemia, gave him her bone marrow for a transplant. Shortly thereafter she was diagnosed with breast cancer and died in 1999.

Growing up in segregated Meridian, Mississippi, Mockbee "had an exceptional education, no doubt at the expense of blacks," he says. The professions, other than nursing and education, were largely closed to women, and so Mockbee's teachers were "mostly women who today would be CEOs." In first grade Governor Ross Barnett's sister was his teacher, and the late U.S. Senator John Stennis's sister taught at Meridian High School. He knew blacks only as maids, caddies, and manual laborers and remained unconscious of the consequences of segregation until a desegregated U.S. Army drafted him in 1966, his junior year at Auburn. During his first weeks at Fort Benning, Georgia, he says, when standing in a line or on maneuvers he would "make sure to have a white person in front of me and behind me. I wasn't afraid of blacks, just had never experienced them as equals." Then one day, he says, he fell asleep in a rifle-range class. "When I woke up, I was in the middle of all these black trainees who were also from Mississippi, and I was fine, in a nest of equals." He went back to sleep, he says, and the "race thing had ceased to exist for me."

It was replaced by a feeling of being both blessed and cursed as a southerner. After 1966, he grew aware that his region "was attached to fiction and false values and a willingness to justify cruelty and injustice in the name of those values." James Chaney, the martyred southern civil rights worker, gained Mockbee's respect and admiration for having the courage to "risk his life and accept responsibility," a message Mockbee translated into a question he has repeatedly asked himself ever since: "Do I have the courage to make my gift count for something?" Although he did not take an active part in the civil rights struggle, Mockbee began to look for ways to help redress the wrongs perpetrated by his kin against "a whole army of people who've been excluded and ignored forever, people who are left over from Reconstruction." A hundred years ago, Mockbee will remind you,

During a design presentation, Mockbee (seated near center) hears students out

W. E. B. Du Bois proclaimed that the twentieth century would be haunted by the fact that Reconstruction was prematurely stopped. "And here we are in the twenty-first century," Mockbee says, "and we're still ignoring the problem and southern blacks are still invisible." He concludes that addressing problems and trying to correct them is "the role an artist or architect should play."

By the early 1980s, the architectural practice that Mockbee had started in 1977 and later shared with Coleman Coker was thriving, but more and more, Mockbee says, he found himself thinking about the Renaissance architect Leon Battista Alberti's injunction that an architect must "choose between fortune and virtue."

An opportunity to opt for virtue presented itself in 1982 in the guise of Sister Grace Mary, a Catholic nun living in Madison County, Mississippi. She enlisted Mockbee's help in moving condemned houses and renovating them for use by poor people near his home city of Canton. That led to Mockbee's first new "charity" house, which was built for $7,000 with donated and salvaged materials and volunteer labor. The clients—Foots Johnson, his wife, and their seven children—were living in a shanty. The 1000-square-foot replacement, a dormered dogtrot, was the precursor of Rural Studio houses. "I learned that small projects like that were doable by ordinary people," Mockbee says.

The experience was Mockbee's first foray into what he calls a "taboo landscape" inhabited by poor southern blacks. "I'd grown up all around it, but I'd never been in any of those houses. I brought friends who helped build that house in a real bad pocket of poverty, and some were pretty politically conservative. But when they crossed over into their world, they got to know them as real people." Racial issues, he concluded, were actually about economic disparities. "When you really get down to it, money talks. Money is thicker than blood. That's one thing I went through in discovering that there's very little difference between people."

Mockbee's firm planned to build three houses for needy families for the nonprofit Madison Countians Allied Against Poverty. The agency selected the families; the designers extrapolated their housing needs. The architects' designs, based on dogtrot and shotgun southern colonials, won an award from *Progressive Architecture* magazine, but then Mockbee's application for a construction grant was turned down. If moneyed people could "just walk into Foots Johnson's house and see him in that taboo landscape, I believe they'd help us in finding financial support and to address these problems," Mockbee recalls thinking. So he started portraying people from the "taboo landscape" in oil on canvas. A grant from the Graham Foundation helped him along. His first subject was the family of Lizzie Baldwin, who had cared for his mother when she was sick with cancer. He saw in that family "an honesty that permits differences to exist side by side with great tolerance

and respect" and tried to convey it in brilliant colors. "The paintings which began the Rural Studio try to establish a discourse between those of us who have become mentally and morally stalled in modern obligations and these families who have no prospect of such obligations," he later wrote in *Architectural Design* magazine. "The paintings are by no means an attempt to estheticize poverty. It's about stepping across a social impasse into an honesty that refuses to gloss over inescapable facts."

A final piece of Mockbee's Rural Studio collage was his 1990 visit to a Clemson University-sponsored architecture program in Genoa, Italy, where he was impressed by the students' camaraderie. He returned home ready to explore the idea of creating a similar project in the American South.

The following year, D. K. Ruth, chairman of architecture at Auburn and a friend of Mockbee, hired him as a full professor. Ruth later became the Rural Studio's protector and advocate at the university. The two men lamented that architectural education had "become more about academics and less about construction," Ruth says. "The connection between esthetics and the realities underlying design was being lost." Auburn did, however, offer at least one hands-on exercise. "We had the students do these little temporary constructions, a beam, a truss. Then they'd be torn down. So Sambo and I thought, 'Man, you could take these materials and build a house, build something substantial.'" Around the same time, three Auburn thesis students told Ruth they wanted to do a design/build thesis project. The department chairman acceded, provided they find financial support and a realistic project. It was not long before they located a house that needed to be restored in the town of Opelicka, Alabama, near Auburn, and convinced the local historical commission to award them a $20,000 grant. With these students' experience in mind, Ruth met to discuss funding with leaders of the Alabama Power Foundation, who proved eager to help the architecture department do something for the disadvantaged rural poor. The Rural Studio began in 1992 with a $215,000 matching grant from Alabama Power.

Mockbee says of his choice of location, "I was familiar with *Let Us Now Praise Famous Men*. But I'd forgotten it was Hale County." He and Ruth looked for a place far enough from Auburn that students would not be distracted by campus life. More specifically, Mockbee wanted a region similar in economic, cultural, and racial makeup to Madison County, Mississippi, where he had worked pro bono in the 1980s. He found that in Hale County, as well as an almost mystical beauty in its forests, hills, and flat farmlands. The county's lack of building codes and building inspectors, moreover, made it a good laboratory. (He insists, however, that the studio restrict experiments with untried building methods and materials, such as waste baled cardboard, to buildings for its own use.)

What cinched Hale County for Mockbee was an offer of a free place to set up shop. The owners of a defunct former nursing home in Greensboro loaned the studio their abandoned antebellum house. When the owners sold the house two-and-a-half years later, local benefactors stepped up. Greensboro residents Virginia and Elizabeth Saft offered the Rural Studio an 1840s Greek revival mansion called Japonica Path. The students and Mockbee lived there for two-and-a-half years "with the family's antiques. Mighty brave of them to let us do that," Mockbee says.

Next was an 1890s farmhouse in Newbern, a hamlet nine miles south of Greensboro. William Morrisette, a successful retired business-man and Newbern native, had moved away but

"always returned. He was interested in our work, thought it would be good for the community to embrace us," says Mockbee. "Newbern has mostly elderly people, and he saw that Auburn's students would bring an energy of youth, some-thing every community needs." The farmhouse, called Morrisette House, is the studio's hub. Second-year women students live there; the men live in tiny, more rudimentary cottages on the property. Designed by fifth-year students—who rent rooms in Greensboro, Newbern, and Akron—the cottages nestle between the columns of a huge shed. Second-year students take Mockbee's watercolor classes in Morrisette's kitchen and in good weather relax on the porch after a day's work. William Morrisette also donated an abandoned 1832 house, called Chantilly, and moved it to Newbern from Greensboro. The studio will renovate it into an administrative center if funds can be found. It will include an exhibition gallery and overnight quarters for visitors, and its computers will be made available to the community. Morrisette also negotiated the deal on purchase of another house, down the road from the other two, which the studio is refurbishing and expanding for use by a new outreach program for students from other schools and disciplines.

The studio's success depends on partners as well as patrons, and no partner is more important than Hale County's Department of Human Resources. Teresa Costanzo, its director until her retirement in 1999, calls involvement with the studio the highpoint of her professional career. It started on a fall morning in 1992: "One of my employees came into my office to say she needed several hundred dollars for repairs to a family's substandard trailer. If the repairs couldn't be made, the children living there would have to be placed in foster care." The department did not have the money. But the same morning Costanzo attended a community meeting about housing at

Anderson and Ora Lee Harris on the porch of their "Butterfly House" shortly after its completion

which Mockbee was introduced. "He was new in town, and I always tell people that one of the few light bulbs that ever went off over my head went off that day." When the meeting was over, she called Mockbee and told him that her department could come up with materials for the trailer repair if the Auburn students could do the work. Mockbee jumped at the idea, and the studio was soon working for Costanzo's department. That relationship gave the studio's efforts legitimacy, Mockbee says. For her part, Costanzo began giving talks to each class of students, she says, "about the county's social needs, about child abuse and why it occurs, welfare and food stamps, so the students could understand the environment they would be working in."

Mason's Bend was the first of Hale County's poorest communities to benefit from the partnership. Home to four extended families or about 100 people, Mason's Bend is tucked into a curve of the Black Warrior River along an unpaved road twenty-five miles northwest of Newbern. The studio began small there, repairing and enlarging shacks and trailers and getting to know the community. Before long, the Department of Human Resources began referring clients in need of new houses to the studio. The department listed needy families, and the students selected one a year. "We presented the cases to the students, and they decided who would get the houses, questioning our staff and visiting every home. They put hours and hours into the decision," she says. "They took it very, very seriously."

Shepard and Alberta Bryant were the Rural Studio's first new-house clients. In 1993, when the studio began work for them, the Bryants, both in their seventies, were rearing three grandchildren in a shanty without plumbing or heating. As the students worked on the Bryants' new house, they developed the studio's lasting methodology. Each house takes about a year to finish. Fifteen second-year students interview the clients to determine their needs. They work up several designs, have the clients select the best one, and begin construction. Specifics such as finishing materials and detailing are left for the next group to work out. Anything built by an earlier group stays, though unbuilt designs can be modified. The need to work in good weather and when materials arrive means schedules have to be flexible. "We're lucky if we standardize the time for a class and stick to that time every week," says instructor Steve Hoffman.

The Bryant House shows the Rural Studio's hallmark use of ingenious building techniques and donated, salvaged, and recycled materials, the inevitable result of meager budgets. Recovered materials give the buildings "a feeling they've been rained on; they look durable," says Auburn's Ruth. Recycling comes naturally to Mockbee. When he was ten, he says, he asked for building materials for Christmas, used them to build a treehouse, tore it down, used them for a fort, tore it down, used them again for a hot rod, tore that up, and built a second tree house. Students examined several low-tech solutions for creating a well-insulated, inexpensive dwelling before deciding to use eighty-pound hay bales for the core of the exterior walls of the Bryants' 850-square-foot house and covering the bales with wire and stucco.

The studio's characteristic modern esthetic was from the start nudged and reshaped by typi-

Mockbee's Cook House (1991) in Oxford, Mississippi, bears an esthetic similarity to Rural Studio buildings

cally southern rural forms and idioms: sheds, barns, and trailers. The Bryant House, for example, is all porch and roof, a steeply raked acrylic structure supported by slender yellow columns. In explaining the esthetic, Mockbee says, "I pay attention to my region; I keep my eyes open. Then I see how I can take that and reinterpret it, using modern technology. We don't try to be southern, we just end up that way because we try to be authentic. When you start to use historic references in a theatrical way, that's when I'm out of here." Almost all studio-designed buildings have exaggerated, protective roofs that appear to float over sturdy walls. Mockbee explains that the region's annual average rainfall is almost sixty inches, "so flat roofs just aren't going to do it." The challenge is different from that of, say, designers in the arid American West who can concentrate more on sculptural forms. Turning a limitation of climate into an opportunity, Mockbee overstates his roofs. He cants them steeply and makes them look almost airborne, as with the Harris House, sometimes called the "Butterfly House" for its wing-spread roof. Although designed by students, the studio's

The roof of the "Tire Chapel," as the Yancey Chapel is sometimes called, rises toward a scenic overlook

buildings are close cousins to Mockbee's earlier work with Coker, such as the Barton, Cook, and Patterson houses, the first two of which are in Mississippi, the last in Tennessee.

Like Mockbee's buildings for private clients, the Rural Studio's work is usually asymmetric and idiosyncratic, qualities that reinforce the quirkiness that attends Mockbee's and the Rural Studio's jumbo roofs. The exterior materials, too, can be as unconventional as the shapes of the buildings. But even the most futuristic constructions look anchored in their neighborhood, because their scale fits and their shapes spring from the local vernacular.

As the Bryant House neared completion, Scott Stafford, a fifth-year student, began designing and building a little round smokehouse for Shepard Bryant. He embedded colored bottles into its concrete rubble walls to admit natural light and made a roof of road signs discarded by the county's Department of Transportation. The project, which cost a mere $140, took Stafford a year to complete and established a model for fifth-year students. Since 1994, up to fifteen fifth-year Auburn students have been

coming to the studio for a year to design and build community-based projects—a community center, a baseball field, a chapel, a boys and girls club. Working in teams, they design and build, but they also find clients, funding, and materials.

The first such project, the Yancey Chapel of 1995, is an open-air pavilion set into a scenic overlook on Morrison Farm in Sawyerville. It is the studio's best-known building, partly because its steeply pitched roof is photogenic, but also because of its unusual wall construction. The students used 1000 surplus tires filled with concrete to form the walls, keeping the chapel's cost to a mere $15,000. On the same property, shortly after the chapel's completion, Jeff Cooper and Ian Stuart designed and built the Goat House, a study in alchemy. The students took an ordinary concrete-block outbuilding that once housed goats, broke through the building's center to create a double-height space, and topped it with a steep, spikey roof reminiscent of the Yancey Chapel. A homely structure became a pleasing one, and showed how one studio building tends to grow from another. The evolution illuminates Mockbee's role. "Our decision to crash through the original roof had to do with putting in a loft," Cooper says. "Sambo didn't think a loft would be needed. But he let us find that out for ourselves."

The Akron Pavilion, consisting of a huge, slanting roof sheltering a brick floor, illustrates, again, the decisive role played by committed patrons. Robert Wilson, an Akron native who returned home after a career in Ohio, gave the land and donated or brokered the building materials: cypress timbers from a nearby marshland, lumber from an unused train trestle, and bricks from a demolished building.

The HERO (Hale Empowerment Revitalization Organization) Children's Center, the first thesis project to meet a broader social need, defined a new emphasis for the studio. Designed and built in 1998/99 by four fifth-year women students, the building, with its one-way mirrored wall, is used by social workers and law enforcement officials to observe, interview, and counsel children who have been abused. Before the friendly, quirky-looking center was built, youngsters had to be taken to Tuscaloosa to be evaluated in an intimidating, institutional building.

The Farmer's Market, completed in 2000 in Thomaston, in Marengo County, was the studio's first venture not only beyond Hale but into public architecture and economic development. For years the town had been trying to incubate a growers' cooperative, and the Farmer's Market was intended to jump-start one. It succeeded. The market's welded steel represents a new degree of difficulty in studio construction. "This is no longer a little wood-frame building. This is commercial construction," says Mockbee, who is obviously proud of the studio's venture into civic projects. He also likes the fact that public projects pose a greater esthetic challenge: "Chapels are easy to make beautiful. The client is expecting you to raise it to that spiritual level. That's not necessarily the goal with a children's center or a community center, though it should be. You're dealing with issues that are more difficult to bring to a level of architecture. It's tougher."

That is true for a 2000/01 thesis project, a boys and girls club in the depressed town of Akron, a once-thriving river town and former railroad junction. "It's even in its nothingness," says instructor Hoffman, but the town's leaders were eager to advance their community. "When we first got here, everyone welcomed us, cooked us food, and then for a while some of them were too proud and didn't understand what we were trying to do," says Craig Peavy, a fifth-year student. Brad Shelton adds, "They didn't know our intentions, so they backed away until we stood up in front of the whole town and said this is what we're doing, this is why we're doing it, we need your help. We

were embraced by the community. The leaders see this boys and girls club as a catalyst they need."

The stunning Mason's Bend Community Center marks a different type of departure for the Rural Studio, an esthetic one. Above thick, low-lying rammed-earth walls, made of local clay and portland cement compacted with pneumatic tampers, floats a folded sculptural roof that is accented along its crest with a wall of overlapping automobile windshields, creating a fish-scale effect. Hoffman says, "It's like you took a piece of paper and folded it up and sat it lightly on these massive walls." When reminded that the community center is yet another chapel-like structure, Mockbee, who is not religious, grumbles, "I don't see a cross in here; I don't see a star of David." In comparing the building to the Yancey Chapel, he says, "The siting is so romantic in Sawyerville, it's all perfect. This is a tougher site, and it's part of the community. This pocket of poverty isn't a place you'd expect to find a sophisticated piece of architecture. I think that's great. I guess it's that, as an architect, I'm intrigued by the unexpected, and as a southerner I'm always for the underdog." Jim Kellen, the director of HERO, eventually wants to use the building as an electronic docking station, or port, giving people in Mason's Bend access to a computerized community network. But there is no money, and the prospect seems far off. Almost as whimsical is Mockbee's hope that electronic equipment linked to a Birmingham hospital will allow the building to be used for diagnosis and treatment. For now the chapel, as it is called in Mason's Bend, is just a chapel, a dazzling one.

The Rural Studio's current emphasis and direction is toward larger, more programmatically and technically sophisticated buildings. At the same time, it is expanding to include an outreach program for non-architecture students from other schools. During the summer of 2000, the studio

Shepard and Alberta Bryant in their "Hay Bale House"

conducted its first ten-week outreach program with seven students, including a medieval history major from Hampshire College in Massachusetts, a master's degree candidate in history and film from New York University, and a medical sciences major from the University of Alabama. Among the projects they worked on were a septic system for Mason's Bend, an oral history of the community, and a basket-weaving studio. The group as a whole built a basketball court behind Mason's Bend's new community center. Auburn's Ruth hopes that eventually the studio will become "an arm of a rural outreach initiative that uses this region as a laboratory, looks at things differently, takes the status quo and shakes it up." He and Mockbee point out

that, although the outreach program has substantial room for growth, the architectural education program does not: its small size makes it manageable and encourages the closeness between students and instructors that is so important to the studio's success. Enlarging the program would not only change its character but also add administrative burdens. Mockbee and his two colleagues are already overloaded.

Criticism of the studio has been sparse. It focuses on the assumption that, since middle-class white students minister to poor blacks, the program must be paternalistic. Mockbee bristles at the idea: "It's a two-way street. We don't judge or ask questions. No one is feeling like anyone is taking advantage of anyone." The studio's work, he says, is an academic exercise; the homework is to build a house. The clients, he says, know they are contributing to the students' education. "There's an honesty that exists here. It's good to see our students respect clients they wouldn't have acknowledged on the street before." Indeed, students talk about their clients with affection and admiration. Josh Cooper, a 1996 graduate, says poor people were an abstraction for him before he began working on the Bryant House, yet Shepard Bryant became a role model for him. "I saw a man who would get up every morning and go fishing, not just for the fun of it but to feed his family and the people of that area. He always had a hot fire going for us in the winter to make sure we were warm." Mockbee, too, looks up to Shepard, whom he describes as "a gentle old man who's had a difficult life by most standards, but he accepts life, lives and lets live. He's not bitter, and he's not mad about anything."

The studio's experience with the Bryants also indicates that it does not impose its ideas on clients. Alberta Bryant says she convinced Mockbee and the students to change the siting of her house, because "I wanted folks to see it." Shepard, explaining that he was too old to climb stairs, vetoed the students' initial urge to design a two-story building.

A definite drawback for clients using the Rural Studio's services is that "everything takes more time," says District Court Judge William Ryan, who is also the chairman of HERO. "You have to understand they're learning as they go. It's a tradeoff." The benefit for Ryan, he says, was a livelier, more imaginative, and much less expensive building than he would have gotten on the commercial market.

More than 350 second-year students and 80 thesis students have now participated in the Rural Studio. So why have other architecture schools not spawned similar programs? Mockbee, who has lectured at architecture schools nation-wide, says almost all have similar curricula and risk-averse faculty. "Most of them dress all in black; they all seem to say the same things. It's become very stale, very unimaginative." If architecture is going to "nudge, cajole, and inspire a community or challenge the status quo into making responsible environmental and social structural changes," he says, "it will take the subversive leadership of academics and practitioners who keep reminding students of the profession's responsibilities." No one, says Mockbee, loves to draw and make models more than he, but model-making and drawings are not architecture. The Rural Studio, he says, takes education out of the theoretical realm, makes it real, and shows students the power of architecture to change lives. "Through their own efforts and imagination," Mockbee says, "students create something wonderful—architecturally, socially, politically, environmentally, esthetically. That's the mission of the Rural Studio. And once they've tasted that, it's forever there. It may go dormant for a while, but at least they've experienced and created something that they're not going to forget."

One main reason the program has been difficult to clone is that, as fifth-year student Andy Olds says, "other schools don't have Sambo." He provides a rare example of hard work, artistic talent, earthbound smarts, tolerance, and empathy. He is especially unusual among his notoriously micro-managing peers for letting students make their own mistakes. "I've learned to trust their resourcefulness," Mockbee says, "to let them push directions I probably wouldn't follow."

Talking about the legacy he hopes to leave, Mockbee singles out "something that's going to have power and live long after my living personality is gone. I'm getting close but I'm not there. I've got to keep cultivating and pushing so that what I leave is as significant as I can make it." That is what makes the Rural Studio transcendent.

MASON'S BEND

NAMED FOR THE bend in the Black Warrior River into which it is tucked, Mason's Bend is neither a town nor even a village. It is a community of four extended families—the Bryants, the Harrises, the Fields, and the Greens—totaling roughly 100 people. Their makeshift shanties and trailers skirt an iron-colored, unpaved road that ploughs through weeds, briars, and kudzu-draped apparitions. A deeply hidden backwater, Mason's Bend comes into view only after you take several turns off County Road 15. "The most important thing about it," Mockbee says, "is it's ignored. I call it a pocket of poverty."

BRYANT (HAY BALE) HOUSE, 1994

THE ELDERLY SHEPARD BRYANT makes do by fishing, hunting, and growing vegetables. He and his wife Alberta and their grandchildren lived in a rickety shack with neither heat nor plumbing but abundant holes that admitted reptile visitors and the elements. "When it rained we had to put our furniture in a corner," he says. When the shack seemed near collapse, he had set out to build a new house, and that is when Hale County's Department of Human Services told Mockbee about his plight. "So we asked Shepard if we could help him," says Mockbee. Today, the finished house rises next to the old shack, a testament to innovation, good will, and progress.

The Bryant House, finished in 1994, was the Rural Studio's first completed building. It established several characteristics that would define the studio's house building program. Most important, says Mockbee, "The goal is not to have a warm, dry house, but to have a warm, dry house with a spirit to it." This attitude, plus an insistence on tailoring each house to specific family needs and using inventive building methods and scavenged and unusual materials, distinguishes the studio's approach from that of other low-income housing programs. The emphasis on individuality and esthetics also limits the number of houses the studio can produce.

Ingenious construction gave the house its nickname, the "Hay Bale House." After exploring and rejecting other low-tech methodologies for creating an inexpensive, well-insulated dwelling, the students selected eighty-pound hay bales for the substructure of the walls. They wrapped the bales in polyurethane, stacked them like bricks, secured the stacks with wires, and slathered the result with several coats of stucco. The outcome: inexpensive, super-insulated walls. The Bryants were skeptical and nervous about the use of hay. Now Shepard Bryant says quietly of Mockbee and the studio, "I believe the Lord sent them by." For many students, working for the Bryants and their neighbors involved serving and befriending people whose sensibilities were foreign to them at first. "I'm hoping that through being exposed to poverty something will sink in; I don't push the political stuff," Mockbee says. "These are nice, normal people," he says of the studio's poor clients. "They don't have a clue how to get out of poverty. I hope that in working with them, the students learn not to be so harsh on people."

The Bryants told Mockbee and his students that they mainly wanted each of their three grandchildren to have a room large enough for a bed and a desk; they also asked for a front porch where they could entertain neighbors and family. They vetoed a two-story scheme as well as the original siting before settling on one story and 850 square feet of living space. In the completed dwelling, three little barrel-shaped niches extend like fingers from the rear of the main interior space, which is organized around a wood-burning stove and has a clerestory window. The Bryants' bedroom, for purposes of privacy, is at the opposite side of the house from the children's rooms and is graced with a stained-glass sidelight.

The Bryants spend much of their time on the front porch. Topping it is a corrugated, translucent acrylic roof supported by exposed beams on a row of pale yellow wood columns on concrete block posts. You will usually find Alberta there in her armchair surrounded by buckets of plants and fish, her husband's catch of the day from the nearby Black Warrior River. When showing visitors the Bryants' home, Mockbee is likely to catnap on the living room sofa while Alberta holds court. "I was glad to get my house," she says. "The children was glad; even the chickens and the dogs was glad. I'm proud of my house." The cost, virtually all of it for materials, was $15,000, a sum covered by grants and donations.

Esthetically, the Bryant House is a deft composition of rugged and fragile materials and opaque and translucent ones. Sturdy and low-slung, the house mainly takes its cues from the region's simple sheds and other ordinary buildings. But its porch—especially if called a verandah—suggests local antebellum mansions. David Bruege wrote in *Mockbee Coker: Thought and Process* that Mockbee's work is "a celebration of the commonplace, even as it exemplifies the highest aspirations of high-art culture, in a gentle and almost mystical mix." The Hay Bale House exemplifies that thought.

Shortly after the house was completed, a fifth-year student, Scott Stafford, designed and built a smokehouse for Shepard Bryant a few yards away. Stafford's thesis project, which Mockbee calls Alabama Ronchamp (after Le Corbusier's famous chapel in France), is a round little structure topped by a curved roof. By constructing the walls with concrete rubble, most of it from a demolished silo nearby and curbs torn up by the state's transportation department, Stafford managed to build the smokehouse for $140. He embedded glass bottles in the walls to admit light and used discarded road signs as roofing material. Bryant, showing off a catfish head in his smokehouse, says, "the light shines through the bottles so it looks like a little city at night."

The Bryants' rickety shack (left in photo) was replaced by the Rural Studio's first completed house (right)

The passage of time between 1994 (opposite) and 2000 (above) softened the forms of the house

By 2000 (above) the Bryants had personalized their porch with tortoise shells, plants, and assorted objects

Three barrel-shaped niches provided bedrooms for the Bryant grandchildren (opposite) while a separate rounded structure serves as a smokehouse (above)

Six years separate the photo of Shepard Bryant at his smokehouse, opposite, and the one above

The living room in 1994 (opposite) and in 2001 (above). Alberta has propped her prosthesis on a couch.

One of three rooms built for the Bryants' grandchildren (opposite) and the main bedroom (above)

HARRIS (BUTTERFLY) HOUSE, 1997

THE TYPICAL RURAL STUDIO client is overjoyed at the prospect of receiving a new, cost-free house, but Anderson Harris, an elderly retired farmer, at first declined the offer. "'No, I don't think I'll take one of those today,' as though I was selling Amway," recalls Mockbee of his first visit to the elderly Harris and his wife Ora Lee. Mockbee explains, "Big white man from Mississippi named Sambo giving something away, saying, 'We don't want to change you, just want to help you.' You'd be apprehensive too." Harris objects, "I wasn't afraid of no white man. I didn't have nothing, and I was scared they'd take what I did have. You understand?" That first day, Mockbee returned to his truck and told a little group of students who had accompanied him, "There isn't an architecture agency on the planet that would build a house for that family. They're almost untouchables. If y'all pick them, you would really be doing something wonderful." The students rose to the challenge, and, with some persuasion, Harris relented. In fact, he relished the design and construction process. "He liked watching the students and helping them," Mockbee says. "The chemistry between the students and the family all happened the way that I always hope it will and know it will." Soon Harris was fixing meals for the students, cooking things he had caught in the nearby woods and fields.

The design of the new Harris House was sparked by Mockbee's observation of the Harrises while working on the nearby Bryant House during the academic year 1993/94. "They lived on their porch, which wasn't probably six feet wide and maybe fourteen feet long, at most. When I visited them, we'd all sit on that porch. I knew the porch was a big deal, and this wasn't going to be an air conditioned house."

The Harrises' 600-square-foot new house is nearly half porch and fully ventilated. The winglike tin roof of the porch, supported by sharply angled timbers, explains the house's nickname, "Butterfly House." The roof's two intersecting rectangles create a 250-square-foot screen porch and make the house look poised for flight. And like a butterfly, it is light and airy. The steeply sloping roof harvests rainwater that goes into a cistern and can be used for toilets and laundry, but the primary purpose of the dramatic roof is to channel cool breezes. In fact, a desire to maximize natural ventilation drove the design: A wall-mounted exhaust fan and operable clerestory windows draw air through the building. In winter, awning-style panels cover the clerestories, and a wood-burning stove keeps the one-bedroom house snug.

To accommodate Ora Lee's wheelchair, the students created an entrance ramp and wide doors and affixed handrails and low fixtures in the bathroom. Costs for the house were kept to about $25,000 (plus $5,000 for the cistern and a wetlands-sensitive septic system) by using tin as roofing material and cladding the building in heart pine recycled from a 105-year-old church that was being razed nearby.

Until the studio completed their house in 1997, Anderson and Ora Lee lived in a shack without heat or indoor plumbing. It remains standing. "I wouldn't let no one mess with it," says Harris. "Only thing I hated about it is we didn't have a bathroom." Today, sitting in his living room, where photographs and clippings cover nearly every inch of wall, Anderson Harris still complains that his new house is smaller than the ramshackle one he used to live in. "Doesn't have room for my things," he grouses. But he is not suggesting moving back or that he does not appreciate his new home's indoor plumbing and the ease with which his wife can move around in it.

The Harrises' former home

In 1997, Anderson and Ora Lee Harris moved from a shack (opposite) into their new house (above)

The fully ventilated porch opens into the rest of the house (opposite, 1997; above, 2001)

A school bus used as a home (above) on the future site of the Mason's Bend Community Center (opposite) was moved to the Harrises' backyard

MASON'S BEND COMMUNITY CENTER, 2000

AS YOU DRIVE THROUGH Mason's Bend on its one dusty, unpaved road lined with rusty trailers and dilapidated shanties, the Community Center stands out as a stunning contemporary apparition. Mockbee describes it as "a windshield chapel with mud walls that picks up on the community's vernacular forms and shapes." Like the hamlet's other buildings, the center hugs the ground. It rests on a broad base of rammed earth, which blends with the iron-colored road, and from the back it could be mistaken for an old barn. Mockbee believes it is "as cutting edge as any piece of architecture that you can find in the United States."

Forrest Fulton, Adam Gerndt, Dale Rush, and Jon Schumann began working on the center as their thesis project in the fall of 1999. While helping finish a house in Mason's Bend, they spent a whole month trying to find a project, says Fulton. "We knew we wanted to work in Mason's Bend, because there's a need and a tradition of doing things there." They thought that building a community building would teach them more and contribute more than building a house and decided on a community center that could double as a chapel. A trailer was being used for church services, and the proposed site, skirting the road, was a natural stopping place for book and health mobiles.

The design was dictated in large part by the site, a triangular piece of land that borders the property of three of Mason's Bend's four extended families and belongs to Anderson Harris, owner of the "Butterfly House." In exchange for the use of his land, the studio moved an old bus, in which one of Harris's sons was living, off the site to Harris's backyard.

What began in design as a closed-in structure ended as an open-air pavilion whose fifteen-by-thirty-foot footprint is similar to that of the old bus. From the start the students wanted "something monumental with thick, low walls, like a ruin," Fulton says. "And we wanted something pristine that would add value to the community, something that wasn't ordinary." The project's rammed-earth walls, pulled long and low to suggest a prowlike form, supply heft, and the folded metal and glass roof provides the desired contemporary look.

The building funnels visitors forward through a narrow entrance, covered by a fold of aluminum, toward a nave topped with a fish-scale glass membrane. The distinction between the raised nave with its gravel floor, and a lower side aisle, covered with black concrete, is articulated by a bend in the roof, which explains the barnlike appearance of the rear elevation.

Like most Rural Studio buildings, the community center is a lesson in resourcefulness. The rammed-earth walls are thirty percent clay and seventy percent sand. The mixture, combined with portland cement, was poured into six-by-eight-inch forms—lifts, as they are called—and compressed with a pneumatic tamper. To create trusses the students cut down cypress trees on land owned by Bob Wilson, an Akron native and studio supporter. They sent the lumber off to be cured and laminated and used left-over timbers to handcraft benches. And because there was no budget for buying glass for the roof, they came up with the idea of recycling automobile windshields. Schumann knew of a scrap yard in his home city of Chicago that holds "pull-a-thons," which allow customers to have anything they can pull away for a song. For $120 he obtained eighty Chevy Caprice windshields. The building's structural steel, meanwhile, was donated by the family of a journalist who had written a story about the Rural Studio. After the deals and donations of materials, the center was built for about $20,000, an amount covered by the Potrero Nuevo Fund of San Francisco.

A work of avant-garde design perfectly at home in its rustic setting, a civic building created by altruistic twenty-one-year-olds for people too poor to pay rent, the Mason's Bend Community Center embodies Mockbee's admonition to "act on a foundation of decency."

A facade of automobile windshields (opposite) partially covers a raised nave and side aisle (above)

The building funnels visitors through a narrow entrance into a space used as both a meeting place and a chapel

Long rammed-earth walls and a tall folded metal and glass roof make striking profiles in Mason's Bend

An adjacent playground makes a backdrop to the center

NEWBERN

YOU CANNOT ARGUE with Jim Kellen, executive director of HERO (Hale Empowerment and Revitalization Organization), when he says, "The biggest thing in Newbern is
the Rural Studio." The next biggest thing in town is a one-story general store, Newbern
Mercantile, known as "GB's" for Gordon Brooks Woods, the owner. Its front porch serves
as Newbern's town square. After passing GB's and the Post Office next door, you have left
downtown Newbern. The population is 254; the topography is flat as a table.

Settled in 1816, Newbern's location in the heart of the fertile Black Belt made it a
wealthy agricultural town in the days when cotton was king. What remains is a handful of churches and warehouses, their sides repeatedly mended and patched into tin
quilts. Newbern is, in Kellen's words, "a very rural, very isolated community" in a
county of 16,870 residents where the average annual income is $13,000. Except for cat-
fish processing and cattle farming, employment is hard to find.

Newbern is where the Rural Studio makes its home. The design studio (opposite),
cattycorner from GB's general store, was once a store itself. Morrisette House, an 1890s
Victorian farmhouse, is where second-year women students live and where everyone
gathers for meals and discussions. Spenser House, an 1890s watered-down Victorian, is
home for the studio's professors and participants in the summer outreach program. An
extension at the back of the house provides an eat-in kitchen and communal room and
offers "a pretty view outback with the catfish pond to the east," in Mockbee's words.
Chantilly began in the 1840s as a four-room cottage. Around 1854 it sprouted flanking
wings and ornate trim and became "Arabesque" or "steamboat Gothic." In 1999, Rural
Studio supporter William Morrisette moved Chantilly from Greensboro to one of his
properties in Newbern and donated it to the studio, which is renovating it.

Mockbee sits in front of GB's, Newbern's general store

A student works on a model of Chantilly (opposite); Rural Studio's 2001 commencement at the amphitheater behind Chantilly (above)

THE BARNLIKE SUPERSHED rises 16 feet and stretches 144. It shelters Pods—cottages where second-year male students live. (Ann Langford, the studio's office manager and de facto house mother decided to house the women students in the more comfortable Morrisette House.) The cottages fit snugly in nine sixteen-foot bays between the shed's timber columns. The Pods are a hodgepodge of materials, colors, textures, and quirky shapes—the ultimate in assemblage. In built form, they express Mockbee's description of his own working method. He characterizes it as continually collaging together ideas and experiences, whether he is painting, creating buildings, or even leading the Rural Studio. Like Mockbee's work in general, the Supershed and Pods' diverse components form a coherent whole: the Pods' uniform size and arrangement in two parallel rows, facing a public promenade, give them the soldered-together look of a street wall with varied facades. It is easy to equate the relationship of the Supershed to the Pods with that of Mockbee to his students, the teacher's loose authority providing a common purpose for his students, much as the Supershed unifies its varied Pods.

Mockbee first thought of tucking housing beneath a large span fifteen years ago at a weekend charette, held at Mississippi State University to develop new ideas for low-income shelter. "I looked out at the landscape and saw sheds built as protection over trailers and agricultural buildings," he says. Mockbee began the project in 1997 by putting four thesis students—Chris Robinson, Barnum Tiller, Thomas Palmer, and Jarrod Hart—to work building a metal-roofed superstructure. Supported by hefty timbers recovered from a former railroad trestle, the Supershed was meant to "keep the rain off something of value," Mockbee says, "and allowed us to be very free and sculptural with the architecture under it." The five little cottages that took shape beneath the Supershed's shelter wear a jumble of materials—old street signs, bits of steel plate, printing plates from the local newspaper, and surplus license plates donated by a county judge. The result is a quirky vernacular esthetic. When completed, it will have nine living units for eighteen students. Mockbee did not have Thomas Jefferson's Charlottesville campus in mind, but when he went to the University of Virginia to teach in 1997, he realized that the Newbern complex, with its promenade edged by two rows of housing, though less sophisticated than Jefferson's in Charlottesville, was similar in principle. Once the first Pod was designed to face the central space, an Alabama "academical village" was born.

As a living arrangement, the Supershed and Pods promote closeness among students and between students and professors. Indeed, Steve Hoffman, James Kirkpatrick, Marnie Bettridge, and David Bonn built the first Pod for Mockbee's use. Three Pods quickly followed Mockbee's, one by Melissa Vernie, one by Brandi Bottwell, and a third by Andrew Ledbetter. In 2001, Andrew Olds, Amy Holtz, and Gabe Comstock completed the so-called Cardboard Pod. It represents an inventive use of yet another type of throw-away material: baled waste corrugated cardboard. Three years earlier, when designing a house for Evelyn Lewis, Mockbee considered using cardboard bales for wall construction and rejected the idea as impractical. But it intrigued Olds, Holtz, and Comstock, who as second-year students had worked on the Lewis House, and they returned to the studio as fifth-year thesis students to study the use of cardboard bales as a building material.

The bales result from a manufacturing process that creates sheets of corrugated, wax-impregnated boards, sizes them for packaging, and then shreds, bales, and compresses the leftovers into layers. Because the cardboard is impregnated with wax to make it water-resistant, it is nearly impossible to recycle and usually ends in landfills. But as a building material, its density assures high insulation values, and the bales—measuring 32 x 28 x 78 inches—can be stacked like huge bricks, which is how Olds and his team built their Pod, in part, he says, "to see how long it holds up." If the Pod proves durable, as Mockbee and the students assume it will, the studio plans to design and build a cardboard-bale classroom at the head of the promenade. It will be the analog of Jefferson's library at UVA, but its esthetic will be forward-looking, "of its time," insists Mockbee.

The Supershed slopes toward three idiosyncratic little buildings—a composting toilet and two showers, one enclosed, one open at the top. Like the larger complex to which they belong, the showers and toilet (the work of Jacqui Overby, Jamie Phillips, and Amy Helman) are a medley of shapes and materials: the toilet, which perches on a concrete-block base containing the composting mechanism, is covered in old license plates, silver side out and arranged like shingles, and is topped by a long, shallow gable. The closed shower, a T-shaped metal structure, stands on a round brick base; the topless shower is in a brick and glass-shard cylinder. Asked why the shower is open to the elements, Olds says, "for the fun of it, I guess."

Pods line up beneath the Supershed

The arrangement of student housing allows for private moments and group activities

Students work in and on Rural Studio projects

The Cardboard Pod (2001) is made from discarded, baled sheets of corrugated, wax-impregnated boards

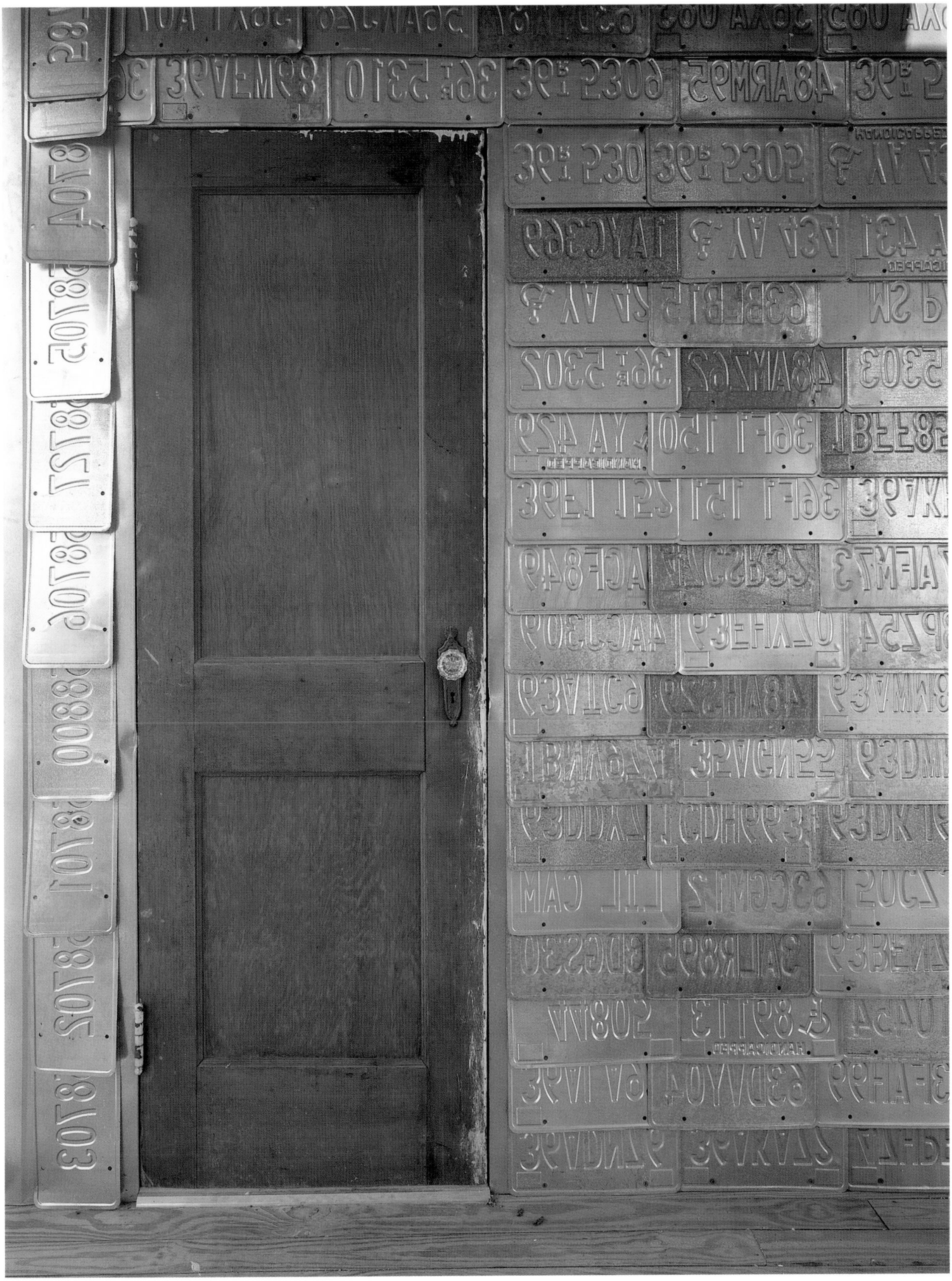

NEWBERN BASEBALL FIELD, 2001

MOCKBEE'S WORK, AT BOTTOM, is about esthetics and ethics. The Rural Studio, he says, "is really about using art to improve people's lives." The new backstop for the Newbern Baseball Club does just that. Lyrically sculptural, it replaces an oft-mended rusty fence and lends dignity and excitement to the popular, decades-old Newbern Baseball Club, home of the Tigers.

The studio's renovation of the field began in a chance meeting in 1998 at the Greensboro Piggly Wiggly. One spring weekend, second-year students Jay Sanders, Marnie Bettridge, and James Kirkpatrick ran into a man they knew as "Tiny," who took them to their first Newbern Tigers baseball game. "We met the team's manager, Major Ward, and were probably the only white guys there," recalls Sanders. "We knew it was a really special place but forgot about it for the next three years." When the trio returned as fifth-year students in the fall of 2000, Ward suggested they think about fixing up the baseball field as a possible thesis project. The existing 1970s frame of the backstop, made by club members of pine and cedar trees cut from the site, was rotting, and its fencing was a chicken wire patchwork.

Sanders saw the old fence as "a beautiful sculpture" and feared "messing this place up." Baseball, explains the fifth-year students' Professor Andrew Freear, "is a very big deal here." The Newbern club, a leftover of the old Negro League, is the largest club in Hale County. "There are ex-players who have been through the Cincinnati Farm system," says Freear. "People come from Birmingham and Atlanta to watch the games." He guesses that a game he attended on July 4, 2000 drew 500 spectators. The games have their familiar ritual. You find the regulars taking the same seats at each game, the vendors in their appointed places selling catfish and fries.

In the fall of 2000, Sanders, Kirkpatrick, and Bettridge presented some initial ideas at community meetings that were attended, Sanders recalls, by Eddie Smith, the fifty-five-year-old ex-pitcher and treasurer of the club; Melvin, who sells scrapple at the games and mows the field; and Washington Turner, an ex-player who wears his old jersey when collecting admission. When the students expressed frustration because they got little feedback from the meeting, Sanders says, "Major Ward told us, 'Y'all just go ahead.' Slowly we started developing a relationship." That helped allay his fear "of messing up," as did the fact that when it came time to take down the existing backstop, Smith and others came out to help.

At first, the students worked on designs for the club independently. Then, as a team, they hammered three concepts into one and began ironing out design problems around a drawing board. "That was hard," Sanders says, "because for years in architecture school we'd worked by ourselves." They won over the members of the baseball club by building a new pitcher's mound and a new home plate, clearing out undergrowth, and seeding and fertilizing the field with help from Auburn's Horticulture Department. The students made videotapes of the field and its activities and began playing baseball with the team. "It slowly became very clear," Sanders says, "that the architecture was not that sacred, that the wood and chain link aren't that important, not even the game. It was the people that gathered here on Sundays, it was the atmosphere created between the cars and the game, the children running around, the old men heckling the umpire, and Susie Lee Williams selling catfish."

Because there was neither water nor power at the baseball field, the students prefabricated the steel structure (the materials for which were donated by the Alabama Civil Justice Foundation) at the Rural Studio's shop. The students fit a "knuckle" on each steel column, from which they extended V-shaped supports. Over this armature they stretched a double layer of chain link that snakes from a high point behind home plate down behind first and third to form, above the knuckle, a sinuous V-shaped gutter that can trap foul balls and roll them toward the sidelines. To stop balls as far from home plate as possible without impeding play, the students created an opening in the fence behind third base. Beyond it the fence has a low "tail." Views of the field are unobstructed, since there are no horizontal members to block sight lines. The backstop shades the stands in late afternoon, game time, and it is glare-free. Because the rusty old fence produced no glare, the students decided to allow the new one to rust naturally. "Hopefully, it'll get better with time," says Sanders.

"There's a lot of the old backstop in the new one," he says. "The parts that we loved, all the falling-over wire, the sagging, flopping look of it we brought back in the new backstop."

Views of the first baseline fence and the dugout

SAWYERVILLE

"IT'S A DOT IN THE ROAD," Mockbee says. Sawyerville lies eight miles northwest of Greensboro on Highway 14, an east-west county road that connects a handful of hamlets, skirting smaller, mostly paved byways. About the size of Newbern, Sawyerville is little more than a post office. The Sawyerville area, on the other hand, has a population of over 2000, mostly African Americans, whose humble dwellings are scattered on the flat land. Eva Bryant-Green, a Sawyerville native who works for the county Department of Human Resources, says, "Life in Sawyerville is slow, casual. You know everybody; you feel safe. A lot of people are related. It's a good place to raise kids. Churches, lots of little churches, are a big part of Sawyerville life." It is here that the Rural Studio built a new house for Shannon Sanders-Dudley.

Sawyerville has its more prosperous, scenic side. There are tree farms, catfish ponds, and pasture land for cattle farming. To Mockbee, Morrison Farm, a dairy farm until the 1970s, "looks like the south of France." Here you will find the Rural Studio's Yancey Chapel and its Goat House. Morrison Farm is mostly rolling meadowlands sprinkled with stands of cedar, sweet gums, and oak—red, white, and live—and there is a catfish pond and a thirty-acre lake for fishing. Lem Morrison, an industrious man with eight years of schooling, built the farm into a thriving enterprise that provided and processed milk and cream for his Dairy Fresh Corporation, a Greensboro-area employer with a reputation throughout Alabama for good ice cream, milk, and other dairy products. Lem's daughter Dr. Lemuel Morrison still raises bulls on Morrison Farm.

IN 1994 MOCKBEE and Ruard Veltman, a fifth-year student, were admiring the light filtering through the bottles embedded in the walls of Shepard Bryant's round smokehouse. When Veltman mentioned that his thesis group wanted to "do something like this," Mockbee replied: "Why don't y'all build a chapel?" Shortly thereafter, Mockbee found himself talking to Lemuel Morrison, whose family members are Auburn University supporters and dairy owners. She offered to let the students build a chapel on her farm in Sawyerville and to help defray construction costs. Veltman and his thesis project partners, Steve Durden and Tom Tretheway, decided to locate the Yancey Chapel on a bluff from which the land spills thirty feet to an open field and wetlands. The view was striking, and there was a ready-made entranceway for a chapel in the form of a long, concrete cow trough with a metal stanchion, a relic from a time when the property was a working dairy farm. The trough forms a rustic allée, which, Veltman says, is in harmony with the "slightly dilapidated look of the chapel. The roof was intended to suggest a caved-in barn structure."

The students' ingenious selection of construction materials and methods allowed them to build the chapel for $15,000. Central Tire Company in Selma, familiar to the students and Mockbee as a landmark on the road between the Rural Studio and Auburn, was under court order to clear its lot and offered to donate its stash of 1000 automobile tires to the project. To form the chapel's walls, the students filled the tires with soil until they became rock hard. It was patient, slow work: at best, the three students could pack only thirty tires a day. To fortify the tire frames, they inserted reinforcing bars, then wrapped the tires in wire mesh and coated them with stucco.

The students scavenged the rest of the materials for the Yancey Chapel. They quarried floor slates from a creek in Tuscaloosa, harvested heavy pine timbers from an abandoned building, and used rusted tin shingles cut into eighteen-inch squares as roofing material. "It's thrown-away tin from old barns and stuff," says Mockbee. The font and pulpit are made of used scrap steel donated by the Hale County Department of Transportation.

Approaching the chapel, a visitor steps down into a narrow, dark entryway to face a pulpit made of found metal materials. A little stream spills through a break in the back wall, trickling over a large slate down into a trough. The visitor steps over it on a metal grill, and the water, a soothing touch, continues its flow to the front of the eleven-by-twenty-two-foot open room and flows to the wetlands below. Typical of studio projects, the chapel reveals itself slowly: "You want to keep the mystery going. You don't want to give your secrets up too soon," Mockbee says. Overhead, to either side of a heavy ridge beam supported by wood rafters, are intervals of sky, then corrugated roofing. The roof lifts as it approaches the pulpit, flooding it with natural light and opening the view.

The chapel comfortably holds about eighty persons. But 300 came to celebrate when Durden and his bride Laura were married in the building shortly after its completion in the fall of 1996. Mockbee recalls that the building was festooned with white flowers, "the priest was in white robes, and this white bull walked by down there in the wetlands."

The Yancey Chapel's narrow, dark entry (opposite) leads to a little stream running into a trough (above)

THE GOAT HOUSE, located near the Yancey Chapel on Morrison Farm, is named for its former occupants, the animals that lived there when it was a concrete-block shed. The Morrisons had planned to transform their farm into an artists' colony. They wanted to convert the former goat house into the compound's hub, a residence and workspace for two artists and an occasional guest house for the Rural Studio. The artists' colony did not materialize. But Jeff Cooper and Ian Stuart remodeled the humble structure into a noble eye-stopper, and the Morrisons now use it as their residence.

Cooper explains that his and Stuart's 1997/98 thesis project assignment "was to move into the house and develop a dwelling and workspace based on our experience of living there." They would learn firsthand what Mockbee meant when he said that "as a social art, architecture must be made where it is and out of what exists there." Cooper and Stuart prowled the farm and became intimately acquainted with it, with the neighboring countryside, and with the county seat of Greensboro, which looks much as it did when Walker Evans photographed it in the 1930s. They found a variety of building materials stored in the Morrisons' barn. "So through collecting these timbers and bringing them up to the goat house and laying them down and figuring things out, we developed the main ideas for the house," Cooper says.

The evolution of the goat house illustrates the studio's typical design/build methodology. After doing preliminary, schematic, and foundation designs, "everything happens on-site," says Mockbee. "It's sort of how architects worked 100 years ago."

The students began by breaking through the roof and creating a double-height dormered dogtrot. They wanted to make a loft until they saw that it would be superfluous. "Somewhere between knocking the walls down and cutting the roof out we realized we'd be insane to drop another ceiling," says Cooper. "It just became this grand space that opened up to the landscape and was so much more powerful than a loft would have been." Mockbee had foreseen this from the start but let the students grasp it on their own.

Cooper and Stuart installed huge wooden doors that, when open, transform the central space into a fresh-air pavilion and frame views of a barn and an ancient oak tree out back. Flanking the central workspace are sleeping areas in the back and a kitchen and living area in the front. Cooper is a talented craftsman who likes to get caught up in details. He clad the walls in tongue-and-groove hard pine, mitered and hand-fitted together all the woodwork and replaced original aluminum windows with hand-milled casements, which he pinned with dowels and glued. "The mortise and tenon and pinning thing is something we did throughout the house," he says.

Viewed from outdoors, the dormered roof tilts up toward the front of the house where oversized wooden rafters provide expressive punctuation. "The roof pays respect to the chapel," Cooper says. The slant of the roof also extends a line formed by a row of raised cattle sheds that "are like the spine of an animal that rides all the way up to the back door," he says. "The roof picks up the hump in the ground and thrusts it forward." The supporting columns were slave-hewn corner columns from an abandoned antebellum house, according to Cooper. They shaped the hoof-like piers in which they are embedded. "Each piece of material started to dictate how it was supposed to be used and connected," he says.

For Cooper one of the most valuable aspects of working on the goat house was Mockbee's "making you feel like you can do anything but letting you come around to the right choices. So much of architecture school has been control freaks, so it's refreshing to have somebody who just lets you see the right stuff. He doesn't force you into it."

The central double-height dormered dogtrot makes a grand space opening up to the landscape

The front living area (opposite) and back sleeping area (above)

"HER STORY TELLS you that she's been serious about getting her life together," says Professor Steve Hoffman about the client for whom his second-year students finished a new house in Sawyerville in the spring of 2001. A decade earlier, Shannon Sanders-Dudley was a single teenage mother. After earning her GED, she found work with VISTA, then with the Hale County Department of Human Resources, and, most recently, as secretary to the county school board. When human resources recommended her to the Rural Studio in 1999, Sanders-Dudley was sinking much of her paycheck into inadequate government housing in a neighborhood where she feared for her six children's safety. The students liked her pluck and her manner: she was "quiet but obviously concerned about her kids," says Hoffman. The students were also swayed by the existence of a building site next to Sanders-Dudley's mother's house; they liked the idea of helping cultivate the children's relationship with their grandmother.

Unlike the Rural Studio's earlier houses, which were small and simple in plan, the Sanders-Dudley residence has a 1500-square-foot ground floor plus a 200-square-foot loft, and accommodates the complex needs of a large family. In planning sessions with Hoffman and the students, Sanders-Dudley came up with the following wish list: a formal entry and dining room, a family room that did not have to be kept neat, a master bedroom away from the children's rooms, and a private place with a window where Sanders-Dudley could snatch quiet moments away from her lively brood. If possible, she said, she would also like a fireplace. She got it all.

The hardest part, Hoffman says, was meeting her request for rooms with formal, traditional uses as well as rooms for casual activities. "That's a middle-class luxury that's not present in any of our other houses," Hoffman says. "The challenge was to design a large, practical house without letting it turn into just another dumb, functional thing you might find in the suburbs." The building's large size prohibited the kind of expressive architecture that made the Butterfly House and the Goat House distinctive. The budget and schedule ruled out extravagance; Hoffman charged the students to keep the design simple but strong and to not "get hung up in architectural gymnastics."

He explains that one of the reasons they chose to use rammed-earth walls was that they, unlike standard wood-frame construction, do not require any finishing. They had other advantages: cost effectiveness, fire resistance, good insulating qualities, and resistance to tornado damage. Besides, the material is beautiful. Successive tampings of the claylike mixture result in a deep rust-colored, rippling surface that resembles a striated rock deposit from successive geological eras. The rammed-earth wall sits on a gray concrete floor slab and is capped by a concrete tie beam, atop which there is rippled tin—"one of our favorites out here," says Hoffman. Beneath the overhanging standing-seam shed roof, finally, are clerestories and infill panels made of a lightweight, durable, and maintenance-free combination of cement and pressure-treated wood fibers.

The building's forms emerged out of its floor plan, a result, in turn, of the students' analysis of how the family lives and of Sanders-Dudley's wish list. The house is arranged like a dumbbell—living spaces at its center, bedrooms on both ends. Approaching from the north, you first see the master bedroom wall with its big bay window. The recessed entrance is around the corner near the center of the long west wall next to floor-to-ceiling French doors. In the central space are a dining room and a combined kitchen-family room, from which Sanders-Dudley can oversee her children's activities. Adjoining the central living area on the south are two ground-floor bedrooms; a full bathroom, a half bath, and a utility room line the back wall. A loft tops the bedrooms, and above the dining room you will find the house's "gem," as Hoffman calls the screened porch.

The house was designed to be cool in summer. The open plan encourages ventilation as do operable clerestories and openings in the roof; the rammed-earth walls are relatively slow to warm up in the summer sun. Completed without heating or air-conditioning, the house came in at about $40,000, and there is room for expansion in the rear.

The Sanders-Dudley House lacks the design magic of the Bryant House and the esthetic verve of the Goat House. It is a workhorse—rugged and broad shouldered—for a big family. Its distinction lies in its low-slung modern shapes derived from vernacular forms and in its combination of natural and industrial, robust and delicate materials. It is far from "another dumb, functional thing."

GREENSBORO AND THOMASTON

GREENSBORO WAS THE HUB of the local cotton plantation–based economy from 1830 until the Civil War. When Hale County was formed in 1867, Greensboro was designated as county seat and has been the area's largest town ever since. Because Northern troops did not torch it when marching through Alabama (the city had little industry to help the Southern war effort), Greensboro and its environs still hold a wealth of antebellum homes and some of Alabama's oldest churches. But the vacuum left by the decline of the cotton economy was never filled. Today, with a shrinking population of 3500, Greensboro remains the commercial center of Hale County. It has developed new industries—milk processing, poultry packing, timber, and catfish farming. But its false-front downtown has hardly changed from the days Walker Evans photographed it during the Great Depression. Local businesses struggle to stay afloat, and HERO's Executive Director Jim Kellen says that the downtown vacancy rate is approaching fifty percent.

Hale's neighboring county to the south is Marengo. Thomaston, located in northeastern Marengo, is urban like Greensboro, despite its population of only 600. It is less impoverished than many communities its size in Hale, mainly because of its location at the intersection of two highways. One runs east-west to other hamlets, the other north to Tuscaloosa and south to Mobile. In and around Thomaston's downtown there are ten or twelve local stores and businesses, including a bank, a laundromat, a mom-and-pop grocery, and a feed store—"just the necessities of rural life," says Mayor Patsy Sumrall. But the majority of downtown storefronts stand empty. People work mainly at nearby paper mills and lumber companies, whose timber-laden trucks are a familiar sight. Apart from the whoosh of cars on the highway, Thomaston stays quiet. "There's a lot of need in a rural community," Sumrall says.

LOCATED IN THE heart of Greensboro, the HERO (Hale Empowerment Revitalization Organization) Playground serves as a backyard for the Hale County Department of Human Resources. Its mounds and valleys are miniaturized rolling hills, made for rolling and sliding. The first design that fifth-year students Melissa Teng and Joe Alcock proposed in the spring of 1997 was flat with conventional playground equipment, a "little McDonalds," says Steve Hoffman. Now an instructor at the studio, Hoffman was a fifth-year student when the playground was created and a friend of the designers. Teng and Alcock began by researching playgrounds and learned that small children seem most comfortable in natural environments. The students brought in truckloads of soil to create mounds. They briefly toyed with a Garden of Eden theme, and then moved on. What ultimately drove the design was their desire to make something special out of everyday components—a large sandbox, a tire swing, and earth-covered metal cylinders through which to crawl.

The HERO Playground, followed by the HERO Children's Center, marked a first step for the nonprofit. Jim Kellen says that to help the poor of Hale County "overcome the historical disadvantage of isolation," his organization wants to expand its "family services mission." The organization owns a large city block of unbuilt land surrounding the playground, which Hoffman is master planning as part of his master's degree thesis. If money can be found, the Rural Studio will design and build a day-care center for HERO.

The only disadvantage of using the Rural Studio, says Kellen, is a "lack of human capital. There aren't enough students to do everything we would like to see done."

BEFORE THE HERO CHILDREN'S CENTER was completed in 1999, mental health care professionals and law enforcement officials had to interview children suspected of being abused in the offices of the Hale County Department of Human Resources. "It's cold, it's sterile in there," says Teresa Costanzo, the department's director at the time. The new center, which she calls warm and friendly, was designed and built by four young women as a thesis project. The department's family resource center, the district court, district attorney, police department, and county sheriff's department use the HERO center for examining and evaluating children. It is also used as a training facility.

The student architects—Allison Bryant, Ginger Jesser, Michael Renauld, and Nikol Shaw—began their work by questioning Costanzo and visiting nearby day-care centers. Their research convinced them the proposed center needed to be inviting and cozy, and that it should separate interviewing and training functions into two buildings. "The classroom had to be very public, but the interview spaces needed to be very quiet, very intimate, and without distractions," says Jesser. The students also wanted the existing Rural Studio-designed playground, which adjoined the proposed center, to be visible from inside the building so that social workers could observe children and parents interacting. Costanzo says the 1285-square-foot setup works beautifully. A big, colorful mural in the interview room disguises a one-way mirror, children and parents can go out to the playground, and the whole visit can be monitored and supervised.

A double-height open dogtrot, covered by a corrugated metal gable that is supported on telephone poles, separates two modest single-story structures and leads to the playground. The dogtrot appears to be a direct offspring of the Goat House. And, as at the Goat House, the roofed dogtrot transforms a common structure into an exceptional one. It was a fluke, says Jesser: Her team's original plan was to close and air-condition the dogtrot, but there was neither time nor money. When they decided to leave the space open and roof it as a shaded breezeway, "That one decision made our project," she says. The result is a building of contrasts: the tall open dogtrot with exposed timbers acts as a foil for two dense, low wooden buildings—one containing an interview room, the other a classroom. Enlivening the center are improvisations, including windows inserted at a tilt and collaged building materials—red-painted wood, natural wood, concrete, and metal cladding and roofing. A metal awning on one side of the dogtrot was recycled from an installation Mockbee's firm created for "Fabrications," a 1998 exhibit at the Wexner Center in Columbus, Ohio.

Jesser says the community "really became involved" in the project. Garbage men stopped by and offered a hand. Prisoners from the nearby State Cattle Ranch obtained permission to help with the construction, and one of them, an expert brick mason, returned to the building after its dedication "to finish the brick flooring in the dogtrot the way he thought it should be done," says Jesser. "It was like he was giving back to the community what he had taken from it." The Pella Corporation donated all the windows, a company in Tuscaloosa gave the students a discount on stain that brightens the interior concrete floor, the Alabama Power Company contributed the telephone poles, and local merchants donated paint and carpeting.

HERO's chairman, District Judge William Ryan, says the students saved his organization a great deal of money that then could be used to deliver services. The building, he thinks, is "much more creative" than what he would have received on the commercial market. One of the great things about the students, he says, is that they are excited about life. "They don't know you *can't* do things, and, therefore, things get done that normally wouldn't." At the same time, he stresses how important it is that students at the Rural Studio are exposed to the realities of Hale County, where "they see there's a different world than the one with fifty-story buildings. They see how people live in this forgotten part of the world."

A double-height open dogtrot separates two modest single-story structures and leads to the playground

The classroom (opposite) and the interview room (above)

THOMASTON FARMER'S MARKET, 2000

THE THOMASTON FARMER'S MARKET, a 1999/2000 thesis project, was the Rural Studio's first foray into architecture to advance economic and town development. In addition to being civic architecture, the market is "citizen architecture, making students become citizen architects," says Mockbee. The student architects—Bruce Lanier, Melissa Kearley, Jimmy Turner, Jay Waters, and Jeff Johnston—found themselves acting not only as designers and builders but also as developers. They had to deal with state and local agencies, including the Alabama Highway Department, and execute the kinds of transactions that can be bypassed when working in rural Mason's Bend or Sawyerville. And rather than being assigned a site, the team members had to find a suitable property.

They chose the little municipality of Thomaston, about twenty miles south of Newbern, over two other contenders, Uniontown and Demopolis. Lanier explains that Thomaston had the required population density—about 400 people, half black, half white—and that its location at the intersection of two highways favored future development. As important, perhaps, the town's officials, including Mayor Patsy Sumrall, strongly supported the project. Her administration saw the Farmer's Market as a potential boost for their struggling town, most notably by helping incubate a cooperative grocery store, which they hoped to develop next to the proposed market.

Mockbee took the new type of venture in stride. Before beginning their design, he says, the students asked him, "What if the town doesn't go through with the coop?" "If it works out, fine; if it doesn't, that's all right too," he said. "Maybe something good will come out of our efforts." The students began by researching similar markets and visiting examples in the region. They learned that most were at a corner or close to one, faced the street, were sheltered by a roof, and were large enough to accommodate farmers' trucks. The proposed location in Thomaston is on a corner that had been leveled by a tornado. One side faces a highway, the other a row of empty storefronts on the intersecting street.

The market is mainly columns and a roof, a butterfly of corrugated metal with a prominent drain at its center. The plan is to plant jasmine to climb up to the drain, "like a tree that makes a sculpture," Mockbee says. The roof's supports—ribbed metal purlins, one-inch horizontal steel piping, and piped steel columns—are all welded. "This is no longer a little wood-frame construction. The sophistication of the projects is increasing," he says. The eight-foot spaces between columns are sized for vendors' tables. Lanier says his team wanted to make the project look anchored but light. Hence the airy roof on columns secured in concrete bases. The columns are fitted with lights encased in metal mesh, which gives the market a nighttime identity. The students also put in a sidewalk and a parking lot and planted trees. The result of the studio's effort is a sheltered space for vendors, a shady area for selling produce from the back of trucks, and a grassy public space for the community.

The community showed great interest in the Farmers' Market, in part because the proposed cooperative would be funded by shareholder equity. "The whole community got loosely involved," Lanier says. "People would stop by, check us out. At first they were a little suspicious." Mockbee advised the students to win over the town through industriousness. It seemed to work. Thomaston's residents began to pitch in, and some opened their homes to students. One night, for example, the mayor invited them in after work, and Lanier remembers scrubbing off the day's dirt and stepping out of the shower to find that Mayor Sumrall had laid out clean clothes for him from her husband's closet. When the market was completed, the whole town turned out with a parade and fireworks.

For the students the market was a political education as well as a design challenge. They had begun with the idea of "creating a dialogue between the Farmer's Market, the coop grocery, and a local canning kitchen business," Lanier says. Thanks in part to the Rural Studio's involvement in Thomaston, the town eventually received help from Auburn University's agriculture and business colleges in developing the canning kitchen business, Mama 'n Em's, a purveyor of canned jellies and preserves and a major shareholder in the cooperative. The students, meanwhile, obtained help from the Alabama Department of Agriculture and Industries, Tuskegee University's Small Farm Outreach Training and Technical Assistance Project, the West Alabama Retail Cooperative, Inc., and Auburn's Department of Rural Sociology, among other entities.

AKRON

AKRON, A ONCE-BUSY river town of boxy, low buildings that huddle beside the railroad tracks, looks like a set from the film *Fried Green Tomatoes*. The town has a convenience store/gas station, a modest town hall, and a few older buildings that used to be hotels, boarding houses, or stores. Its downtown is brick and cinder block, and few of Akron's buildings rise above one story. When the Rural Studio was building the Akron Boys and Girls Club in 2000/01, "the fact that it would have a mezzanine, that alone created excitement among the kids," says Patrick Ryan. He was one of three fifth-year students who designed and built the club.

In the days when transportation meant railroads and shipping, Akron prospered because of its location on the Black Warrior River and because it was the only place between New Orleans and Birmingham where a train could be turned around. But when cars and trucks took over, the town languished. "Not being on a highway between two other points means you want to be in Akron or you're lost," Ryan says. "There are no people stopping by. That hurts the town economically." Nearly all of its 600-odd residents are African Americans who live in trailers raised on blocks in case the Black Warrior floods.

WHEN BOB WILSON, an Akron native in his sixties, came home to retire after spending his adult life in Cleveland working for a railroad, he wanted to improve his depressed little hometown. One of his first ideas was to create a place for community events, maybe for family reunions. In 1996, he hooked up with three eager thesis students—Steve Hoffman, Jon Tate, and Todd Stuart—and donated deeply wooded land that had belonged to his grandfather, a lock tender—land adjacent to the Black Warrior River. During construction of the Akron Pavilion, Wilson became a "fourth team member," according to Hoffman. "He was on the site with us every day, digging the foundations, pouring concrete," and he and his grandson helped obtain salvaged bricks for flooring.

Like many Rural Studio projects, the Akron Pavilion began with the student architects wanting to incorporate everything they knew into the design. In the end, the materials at hand gave the structure form. "We didn't have a realistic picture of what we could accomplish," says Hoffman. Around Christmas time, he recalls, during faculty criticism of the team's initial design, "the professors were telling us, 'You've got to get rid of this and this and this.' Then we had a rainy January, which fortunately kept us from starting construction and gave us a chance to redesign." Even after they began building, the team changed the design in significant ways: they further simplified it, reduced its size, opened it up to the elements, and eliminated an auxiliary structure. "It happens a lot," Hoffman says. "The necessity of the situation made us rethink what was important."

Crucial for the pavilion's design was a railroad company's donation of ties and other building materials. "That appealed to us because it was the train that took Bob Wilson away from Akron, and the train is a really significant piece of the history of Akron," Hoffman says. Akron owed its once-thriving economy to both river traffic and the railroad. Recycled timber columns and beams from an outdated railroad bridge gave the students inspiration. "We said, okay. This is what we have to use. The design [came to us] one thing after another like that," he says. Because the pavilion is in a flood plane, the students placed concrete pads, measuring four feet square and a foot thick, beneath each column as stout shoes to distribute weight and prevent the columns from shifting. The concrete and brick floor surface is "very beefy where it touches the ground," Mockbee says, which no doubt is how the pavilion has survived two floods.

The shape of the roof emerged from a desire to create something that "wasn't a church or a chapel but could feel that way and that wasn't a performance space but could be used that way," says Hoffman. From the south, the roof takes on the appearance of a high-gabled church, but head-on it is more like a theater's backdrop. "We liked the way the pavilion looked from the road. At first glance it could be an old barn tucked into the woods," says Hoffman.

Mockbee describes the structure, which cost approximately $15,000, as "so rational, closer to being an engineered building. There's an economy of design and construction that's quite beautiful. But it doesn't relax itself. It's just a huge slanting roof and a floor."

AKRON BOYS AND GIRLS CLUB, 2001

IF YOU HAD BEEN THERE one early April afternoon in 2001, when Craig Peavy, Brad Shelton, and Patrick Ryan were completing the Akron Boys and Girls Club, you would have found three townspeople taking turns barbecuing pork ribs for the students and working on construction. When Bob Wilson, whose family donated the former grocery store in which the students were building the new club, was not tending the ribs, he was helping level a concrete sill. Mr. Billy and Monkey Man, as the students call the other two local men, helped pour the concrete floor. While the students worked on the project, they lived in Akron, about a mile and a half from the building site, in a trailer they rehabilitated. Surveying the operation, the students' Professor Andrew Freear remarked, "This is the closest you can get to community architecture." He contrasted the town's involvement in the club's construction with that of "so-called community architecture that is driven solely by architect-developer motives."

What prompted the Rural Studio to create a boys and girls club for Akron? The little town's adults work mostly in Tuscaloosa, thirty miles to the north, or in Greensboro, a twenty-minute drive to the southeast. As Akron has no market, they often take time to shop on the way home. This means most children are footloose from the end of school at 3:30 until 6:30 or so. Hence the need for a supervised place with activities. The students hoped that reusing the former grocery, which fills a triangular site at the town's busiest intersection, would spark a rebirth for Akron. Today, the club is the most prominent and distinctive structure in town.

By the time the Rural Studio arrived on the scene, all that was left of the former store was its beautifully weathered red-brick husk, spackled with ancient blue and green paint. The students decided to retain the walls untouched—except to clean them—to top the structure with a slanted roof, build off-kilter interior walls, and create a metal-wrapped add-on containing a small classroom, a computer lab, a bathroom, and a utility room. "The notion," says Freear, "is the new emerging out of the old." Esthetically, the "heavy hit," as the studio calls it, is the slender roof plane contrasting with heavy blue steel trusses.

The steel framework for the roof—$25,000 worth—was donated by James Turnipseed, an Auburn alumnus. After the students selected steel at his factory in Birmingham, Turnipseed's company reengineered it for them, and they persuaded Shelton State Community & Vocational College, near Tuscaloosa, to reweld its ends. The college's truck-driving program then delivered the steel to the site, and the students fit it together like a kit of parts. Today, at twilight, the lights inside and the blue metal frame transform the structure into a blue lantern behind warm brick walls.

An outsized bay window overlooking Main Street calls attention to the club's presence in the center of town; it turns the interior into a stage and brings the town inside. To add urbanity, Andy Olds, Gabe Comstock, and Amy Holtz, all 2000/2001 fifth-year students, created a canopy and street furniture made of cardboard bales that were sprayed with Shotcrete. Their creation extends the side-street wall and reinforces the path between the town's launderette and gas station.

The Akron Boys and Girls Club and the earlier Akron Pavilion have at least two things in common: both owe a debt to Wilson's generous contributions of property and labor and both have big, distinctive shed roofs. More striking, however, are the buildings' differences. They tell a lot about the Rural Studio's evolving direction. Most obvious, of course, is that the pavilion, hidden in the woods on the banks of the Black Warrior River, is deeply rural, while the club is an ambitious urban project. The pavilion, moreover, "just a huge, slanting roof and a floor," as Mockbee describes it, is the studio's simplest and least idiosyncratic structure, while the club is among its most complex. The decision to top weighty, angled walls with a slender, sloping roof plane made it one of the studio's quirkiest.

The most difficult aspect of the project, says Freear, was fitting a new building within the old walls. Unanticipated "small matters," he says, such as leveling the top of the old wall and connecting new clerestories to it, taxed the students' ingenuity and schedule. The club is also the studio's first fully sealed and air-conditioned space. The HERO Children's Center's two small rooms have central cooling, but they are two little boxes. The club, by contrast, is an open 1500-square-foot volume, and its air-conditioning was installed not by a contractor, as at the center, but by Shelton's father, who obtained a license for the purpose. In addition to dealing with relatively complex design problems, says Freear, the students undertook the complicated task of ensuring the club's future. They contacted its umbrella institution, the Tuscaloosa Boys and Girls Club, and, aided by Wilson, created a board of directors and searched for someone to run the club.

Surveying the students' work on that April afternoon in 2001, Mockbee was heard to say, "Isn't working like this what architecture students should be doing? The Rural Studio is all about people in the final analysis. It's about being decent and trying to provide a decent community for all citizens. It's about being democratic."

The new club sits inside the walls of the old grocery

Though subdued during the day, the building glows like a blue lantern at twilight

Mockbee with students at Newbern design studio, 1997

RURAL STUDIO AT WORK

INTERVIEWS WITH STUDENTS, A TEACHER, AND A CLIENT

JENNIFER STANTON

SECOND-YEAR STUDENT, 2000

During her fall semester at the Rural Studio, Jen Stanton usually could be found on a construction site in Sawyerville. Stanton and fifteen other second-year students were building a house for Shannon Sanders-Dudley and her six children. On the job one hot October day, Stanton put down her hammer and nails to talk about her brief time there. She was attracted to the studio, she says, by "the opportunity to design something and actually see it come to life, be used, and be part of a community." Former Rural Studio students confirmed her initial decision to participate. "The first thing out of their mouths was, 'it's the greatest thing. You've got to go.' Then came stories about interactions with the community and about how close you are to your professors and how much fun you have."

Stanton's very first experience at the studio was memorable. The assigned task was to help fifth-year thesis students build a little cottage, or "pod," for one of the second-year men to live in. "It was an ice-breaking thing," she recalls. "We got to interact with the thesis students and create a family atmosphere. They shared what they'd learned. I think of them as models for us architecturally and socially. When you're in second year, you're still trying to figure out how to design a building. Seeing how far the thesis students have come made me confident that my design abilities will develop. When we go to community events and see the way fifth-year students talk to people who live around here, it's really impressive. That pulls us along."

Construction work on the Sanders-Dudley House was eye-opening. "Usually it's paid laborers doing this stuff," she says, "and we didn't know until we were here how much time and effort they put into it. This work is making our designs become simpler. They're more functional than studio work by Auburn students who haven't been here. We're not putting in a lot of extravagant things like we did before." Working construction has also taught her that a built design often feels different and functions otherwise than she imagines in a drawing. "A five-foot space isn't the same in your mind as in reality; your mind can play tricks," Stanton says.

Another first for her was working as a team and learning the importance of compromise. "I never had to do that," she says. "The interaction among all of us, it gets us thinking." But her team accomplished less than she had hoped because everything took longer to build than she had expected.

Stanton and her female classmates live at Morrisette House, an 1890s clapboard farmhouse; their male counterparts occupy pods nearby. The young women double up in rooms and all share one-and-a-half bathrooms. They have heat and air-conditioning, "when it works." Television is not allowed, Stanton says. She works three full days a week and has classes the other two. On workdays, she and her classmates meet on-site, sometimes as early as 6 A.M. The students return home around 5:30 and, after dinner, scatter to work on renderings, watercolors, and other studio projects. Monday mornings are devoted to classes in materials and methods, Thursday afternoons to architectural history class, which means visiting antebellum houses and drawing their floor plans and elevations.

In late winter, after returning to Auburn at the end of the semester, Stanton reflected that the studio provided exposure to a level of poverty she had never experienced either in her hometown of Chelsea, Alabama, outside of Birmingham, or in visits to her mother's family in Kentucky. "It's kind of amazing that the kids live in such a state but keep smiling all the time," she says. The semester showed her that "life is not about money. It's all about where you put your importance."

Stanton's main regret was that her group had very little contact with the client. "We saw Shannon once or twice, but the previous class got to work with her to figure out most of the design." By the time Stanton arrived, Sanders-Dudley had a full plate, with a new marriage, six children, and a job; the studio was deluged with visits from media and donors; and "the end of our term snuck up too fast. I'd like to go back and say hi to Shannon and have her know I was one of the people who worked on her house."

Stanton values most her close contact not only with thesis students but also with instructors, especially Mockbee. "He's a friend, someone we look up to, definitely, but he's not someone who towers over us," she says. "He's just one of the guys, real comforting. He's brilliant. Little things: he'll compare the elevation of a building to a painting, and that'll get us thinking about composition."

Not surprisingly, the rigor of the Rural Studio was hardest for her, and it is what she misses most. "We lived, breathed, slept, and ate architecture school there. We didn't have a break from it. It was hard to juggle everything that we had to do. At the studio, home is school and school is home. It's a lifestyle; it's not just education. You didn't have life's distractions. It was nice to be able to lose myself in something I love and not have to worry about the rest. That was absolutely wonderful."

Asked if she intends to return to the Rural Studio as a thesis student, she says, "definitely."

ANDREW OLDS

SECOND-YEAR STUDENT, 1998

FIFTH-YEAR STUDENT, 2000/01

Andy Olds spent an entire academic year exploring the potential of baled corrugated cardboard
as a building material and constructed a "cardboard pod" to live in beneath the barnlike
Supershed a few hundred feet from Morrisette
House. Listening to Olds talk about his thesis
project is hearing a man in love with unorthodox
building materials.

When he was a second-year student at the
studio and helped build the Lewis House, Olds
became intrigued when Mockbee briefly considered using waste cardboard as a building material. Mockbee rejected the notion, but Olds and
two classmates, captivated by the idea of recycling a material that usually ends in landfills,
decided to explore the possibilities of waste cardboard as their thesis project.

Olds and his partners, Amy Holtz and
Gabe Combstock, began with the conviction that
since cardboard bales are very dense and have a
high insulation value, "they could be load-bear-
ing and keep a structure cool in the summer and
warm in the winter." And because the 700-to-
1200-pound bales can be easily stacked, Olds
foresaw a future for them as a "fast, easy construction method for low-cost housing." Building
a foundation for the pod persuaded Olds and his
partners that baled cardboard refuse might prove

useful in earthquake-proof construction. The
material creates a flexible foundation, and, Olds
reasons, topping it with a concrete ring beam
should compensate for differentials in settlement
and, by structurally separating the slab from the
foundation, provide the building with more give.

A few feet from the Pod, experimental
bricks are stacked in rows. Made of wax-impregnated cardboard mixed, in varying combinations,
with sand, water, and portland cement, the bricks
show what happens when cardboard is mixed
with other materials. Olds hopes the tests ultimately will yield inexpensive, lightweight bricks
or tiling. Near the bricks lies the carcass of
another experiment, a bale of smoldering cardboard set ablaze to see what fire does to it.

Olds says the studio beckoned him during
his second year because he wanted to build and
liked the idea of taking a break from Auburn
and living in a "big antebellum house. It was
glamorous." At the time, the studio was head-
quartered in an 1840s Greensboro mansion.
Olds's work on the Lewis House was "kind of
frustrating," he says. Bad weather kept interrupting construction. "We didn't feel like we got a
whole lot accomplished." But by the time he left
the studio, "Sambo had made me understand
that where things come together provides a
'detail opportunity.' He taught me about economy of materials, to compose a building without
excess." Not incidentally, this middle-class
youngster from Wetumpka, Alabama, near
Montgomery, learned to enjoy "being able to
hang out with really poor people. At home, you'd
drive down the street and see a bum and keep
driving, but here in Hale County you meet poor
people and learn that underneath they're not
much different than you and me. We [the stu-
dents] stand out like sore thumbs here. It's
important that we're respectful and polite."

Any changes in the second-year program
since he went through it three years previously,

in 1998? It is larger now, he says. There had been eight students in his group; now there are twelve. Before, "the students were almost left to themselves. Now we have [professors] Steve and Andrew, who are really helpful. The studio's organization is improving."

The fifth-year program is less structured than second-year's. "We have a lot of freedom," Olds says, "but every two or three weeks we present our ideas to Sambo and our professor Andrew [Freear]. We have reviews and get feedback. Also, the thesis group is like one big team, and we give each other feedback all the time. Even though Sambo doesn't direct us with a heavy hand, we have a lot of people making sure our designs are good." Olds says considerable learning happens "through doing" and from other students' mistakes. The Pod designers soon learned, for instance, that "since there's no air-conditioning, you'll want a window right next to your bed, not two feet away where some of them are."

Olds continues, "Something Sambo's teaching me now is to be clear and concise when I speak, because he's so busy. That makes me clarify my thinking." Olds thinks that building has taught him to manage time better, "because you have to think and plan ahead in buying materials and having tools ready." He says he learned the importance of taking risks, being flexible, and that "if you want to make things happen, you can't worry about who gets the glory. Sambo teaches that through example. I want to be like Sambo. He sticks his neck on the line and trusts us. I'm amazed that he's so successful yet so humble. He doesn't treat anyone as though they're below him."

Perhaps most importantly, the studio has impressed on Olds the need to believe in what he is doing.

STEVE HOFFMAN

FIFTH-YEAR STUDENT, 1996/97
INSTRUCTOR, 1998–PRESENT

Steve Hoffman was a fifth-year thesis student at the studio in 1996/97. After graduating and working on a farm for a year, he returned to the studio as an instructor and has been in charge of the second-year students since. One October evening in 2000, over a pizza in Greensboro, Mockbee described the twenty-six-year-old Hoffman as "wise for his years, a natural teacher. He's got the right disposition, talent, energy."

Hoffman, a patient shepherd to his flock of students, spends much of his time supervising construction. They are building Shannon Sanders-Dudley's house. "It's good getting out here, getting a little dirty, doing something with your own two hands, seeing the results," he says. The previous class had assessed the client's needs and done the programming; Hoffman let his students' design imaginations run wild before a budget was set. Then, with Mockbee's and Hoffman's help, the students meshed the best ideas and established square footage based on a budget of about $45,000. This morning, a new team is articulating windows and partitions. "They all get to leave their mark on the final product," Hoffman says. "We're trying to give all students a variety of experiences." And as a place of learning, he believes the studio gives him a chance to teach what he believes in.

He is guided by a sturdy social conscience. His parents, after court-ordered school desegregation in their adopted state of Louisiana, sent their son to second grade in a previously all-black school in Baton Rouge, where he remained enrolled until high school. "Working intimately with poor people in Mason's Bend was not a big adjustment or surprise," he says. "For some students it is."

He was drawn to the studio as a fifth-year student, because, he says, by the end of fourth year, "I'd got disillusioned with studio. I'd got all out of it that I could." He says he was disciplined but knew his facile designs lacked grounding in reality. He wanted to build, and his conviction that architecture should have social content struggled against what he regarded as the academic studio's self-indulgence. The Rural Studio "seemed to offer a solution to my dissatisfactions," he says. He learned from Mockbee "to work from a specific, to draw energy and inspiration from the people I work with and the place I work in." He was also inspired by the example of Bob Wilson, the Akron, Alabama, native who, wanting to give something to his community, donated land and materials for the Akron Pavilion, Hoffman's thesis project, and did construction work alongside the students.

By the time he finishes his master's degree at the studio, Hoffman observes, he will have been in Hale County for a full seven years. "So this is as real as anything's ever been in my life." Being there, he says, has made him "more serious about what gives me real satisfaction. I don't have to question if what I'm doing is worthwhile. I'd love to be an architect-builder in a small town doing community-based social service projects and teaching. The more you root yourself in a place, the more you can be an advocate to get things done." He recently bought a house in Newbern.

"Students generally have the ability and intelligence to do what looks and smells like architecture," Hoffman says, "but they learn all the conventions first, building models and making drawings. I try to teach it differently: Conventions like model-building are a means to get someplace, not an end." The best projects, he says, evolve through the process of building. The Mason's Bend Community Center got off to a slow start, Hoffman says, and then "somewhere things began to click. The design went through so many iterations. Sambo just kept pushing them. The same thing happened with our Akron Pavilion." One thing you learn, he says, "if you really want to be brilliant and innovative out here, you have to do things differently rather than better than everyone else. Improvising is one of the lessons of the Rural Studio." Hoffman challenges his students to examine the roles of architects and their work: "Not only how do you go about doing it, but also what does all the stuff I learn have to do with anything?"

The main influence on his teaching is Mockbee's example. "He can find ways to bring out the best in everybody. He's a real light touch," says Hoffman. "He's not dogmatic, but he doesn't let people take advantage of him. He's very good at the one-on-one."

One of the hardest things for Hoffman "is accepting the slowness of the building process, the fact that you have to give the students enough room to screw up, because that's part of the learning process. In teaching you have to have a lot of flexibility."

Sometimes he worries about the Rural Studio's ability to maintain its integrity as a bootstrap individualized operation as it grows and attracts media attention. "We spend more and more time talking into tape recorders," he says. "CNN crews coming down to Mason's Bend is surreal. I'm an idealist, and I'm young. But Sambo's taught me that you also have to work within the non-ideal world."

159

EVELYN LEWIS

A CLIENT

Before Evelyn Lewis and her four children moved into the house designed and built for them by the Rural Studio, family members had been separated. The authorities had condemned the decrepit trailer they lived in and demanded that they move into more suitable quarters. Lewis says her trailer was old when she bought it in the mid-1990s, and after two or three years it was "rotted out and the electricity didn't work." She had no money to fix it. "In the job I had just started I was making really low wages," she says, "like $60 every two weeks." She searched for help. A nonprofit organization promised to assist her to weatherize the trailer, then reneged. The housing authority in Tuscaloosa offered aid "until they discovered I'd been to bankruptcy court." Lewis refuses to name the agencies that turned her down, "not wanting to put folks on the spot," saying only that institutions "designed to help me couldn't do so."

Because she was unable to renovate her trailer, "my family was spread out everywhere," says Lewis. Her oldest son moved to Lewis's mother's house, Lewis's sister took in Lewis and her daughter, and Lewis's two younger sons moved in with her estranged husband, a man with a drinking problem.

Her luck changed when Lewis turned to Hale County's Department of Human Resources in 1998. By then, the department was working with the Rural Studio, providing it with lists of people who needed houses. "This lady at DHR, Melissa Gentry, she told me about the things this organization and its students were doing to help people like me," says Lewis. "She sent the people out to meet me, and I talked to the students and Sambo and Steve [Hoffman], and they told me what they could do for me. They talked to me and my children. They wanted to know what was going on with us and found out that the complaints my husband made about my mistreating my children were unfounded. They said they had many people on a list for a house and they had to choose one family on the basis of how bad their situation was. I praise God that through a lot of prayers they chose me." The studio selected Lewis in large part because she "was very active about doing whatever it would take to rectify her situation," says Hoffman.

Once chosen, she and her children got to know the students. "We had many dinners," she recalls. "They showed me other houses they had built, and they asked me what I wanted in a house. They told me I should not just agree with what they did but tell them what I wanted." Topping Lewis's list of priorities, she says, were high ceilings, "because I'm kind of claustrophobic, you know. I told them I liked lots of windows. And I told them I wanted something that could be for me and my family to get together. I got all that."

The outside of the wood-clad Lewis House is comely but ordinary. A budget crunch and a narrow site produced what Hoffman describes as "almost a trailer but a permanently built one." It is just 1100 square feet in four bedrooms, a small kitchen, a small bath, and a living room that pokes forward. But the house is air-conditioned and the hallway along the south wall has clerestories to vent hot air and a window at one end to encourage cross ventilation. To make up for forced reductions in the building's size, says

Hoffman, the students "wanted to put a lot of effort into the interior craftsmanship, and so the inside of the Lewis House probably has the highest level of detailing of all the charity houses." Among the special touches are patterned tiles in the kitchen and bathroom and press-board wainscoting in the living room.

Lewis now has a better-paying job as a Head Start school bus monitor. Asked what she likes about the house, she says, "I love the way it smells, the looks of the house. The wood is beautiful." How did the students treat her? "With utmost respect. They were very, very nice people."

Did the experience change the way she viewed her world? "You know, I grew up thinking I wouldn't be able to have this and that," she says, "because when I was coming up we were really poor. I thought stuff like this happened only in dreams. Even when the students were working I didn't think I'd get a house; I thought it was just a story. That's why I call it my house of miracles."

"When people just do stuff for other people, you think they're not doing it for the love of people but because of a job. That's not how it was, especially with the girls. They told my daughter they do it to see the smile on people's faces. That's what threw me, because I thought they're just doing a job, trying to get a grade. It wasn't like that."

Portrait of Samuel Mockbee (2001) in front of The Children of Eutaw Pose Before Their Ancient Cabins, *1992*

IN PRAISE OF SHADOWS

THE RURAL MYTHOLOGY OF SAMUEL MOCKBEE

LAWRENCE CHUA

WHEN HERNANDO DE SOTO embarked on his civilizing mission through what would later become the American South, he left behind a trail of misery that extended from Florida to the eastern edge of the Rocky Mountains. Accompanied by priests, de Soto and his men burned their way through native villages, enslaving local citizens in iron neck collars and chains to work as beasts of burdens. The expedition was hungry for wealth, and when one slave fell from exhaustion, de Soto would behead him so as not to impede the progress of the journey. However, de Soto's expedition was slowed down in 1540 by Tuscaloosa, the Black Warrior, king of the Mobiles. Historical accounts describe the Black Warrior as a man of gigantic stature, a commanding eminence who died, along with 11,000 of his subjects, in an intense battle with de Soto's forces.

The Black Warrior River that winds along the western edge of Hale County, Alabama, takes its name from this decimated king. It flows from Bankhead Lake as a thin line and then opens into a thick-waisted body of water. Rivers like the Black Warrior are always somehow larger than life. They move like time, carrying along everything in their drift; they dry up and overflow and, like the history whose relentless current they suggest, constantly change shape. The land through which the Black Warrior curls is rich

with defeat. One has only to kick at its red surface to detect the layers of hurt beneath it. Yet, there is a loveliness to the place that may come in part from the conflicting myths of freedom that shadow its soil. In the paintings, collages, drawings, and architecture of Samuel Mockbee, these shadows implicate everything living under them.

The shadows in Mockbee's work are not immediately apparent. They are often dispersed by the sunny countenance of his buildings, or the bold colors that Mockbee uses in his paintings, or even the ways that the Rural Studio project is discussed. But to see how those buildings are lived in! Those well-lit spaces have been reclaimed and made blissfully dark again. So, too, is the brightness of Mockbee's paintings misleading. To spend time with them is to see that those rich blues and yellows are built up of layers of darkness, the product of a darkness in which life is lived.

In these shadows, Mockbee has created a rural mythology. A place akin to William Faulkner's Yoknapatawpha County, it is a living fiction in which Mockbee's architecture, his wealthy clients, the projects of the Rural Studio, and its poor clients are interwoven with one another. This mythology is a work in progress. It is a process that continues to unfold as personal memories intersect with public histories and the poor and the black become Black Warriors, mother

ABOVE: Alberta's Ascension, *1999*

OPPOSITE: Apple, *1998*

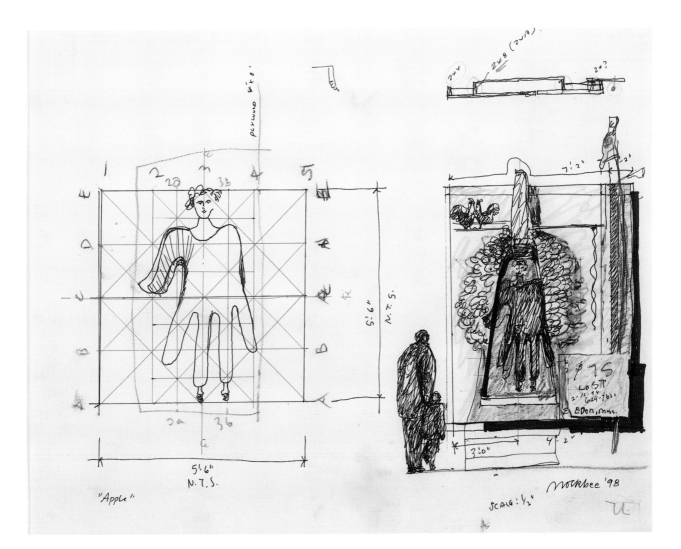

"Apple"

Mockbee '98

SCALE: 1/2"

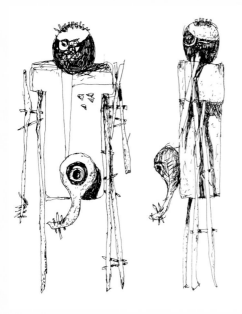

ABOVE: Charles W. Moore Silhouette Sketch, *2001*

OPPOSITE: Untitled, *1991*

goddesses, master knots of fate, ciphers endowed with an agency that allows them to throw their sex hundreds of yards across a lake. In Mockbee's paintings, a man named Web Duboys becomes a demigod named W.E.B.B., a mystical shadow of the visionary intellectual W. E. B. Du Bois. His paramour, Bertha Baldwin, becomes a mother-goddess named Eutaw, the capital of neighboring Greene County. In *Alberta's Ascension* (1999), a woman bound to a wheelchair alights on the back of a giant turtle. If one cannot live a dignified life in history, these paintings seem to ask, can one have dignity in mythology? Is the freedom of history the same as that of mythology?

It would be misleading, however, to suggest that Mockbee's rural mythology is merely a symbolic register. Samuel Mockbee is the first to point out that he was trained as an architect and not as a painter, and he approaches his paintings, drawings, and collages not as a painter always

does, but as an architect should. His work is both a shelter and a mirror.

To paint something is to bring it inside. Between the time of de Soto's expedition and the invention of photography, painting was a way of making meaning of a changing world. In its surfaces, everything became an object. Sights became things. The riches that de Soto sought in the Americas were rendered by European oil painters for the wealthy patrons of imperialist ventures. The lands they owned, their bounty, and the slaves that worked them all were rendered in oil and brought inside. Painting interiorizes the world. It creates an interior space in which meaning is placed. In that space, appearance and meaning cease to be separate categories. The exterior of the world and the interior of the viewer coincide, however briefly. The viewer achieves an equality with the visible and, in that moment, is no longer excluded from the visible world, but is instead at the center of it.

Samuel Mockbee's art is an art of witnessing. Architecture witnesses the events that happen inside it, around it. A painting witnesses too. It safeguards the experiences of memory and revelation. The painting shelters what has been seen by the artist. If the artist has been a good and reliable witness, then the painting shelters the truth. Mockbee's visual work does not witness in the way that images are often called on today to represent things. Instead it proffers a braver acknowledgment of the way the world works. In *Untitled* (1991), a collage, a female figure surrounded by children points to a man hanging from a tree. An electric chair sits in the space that separates them. A ladder rises above the woman's head, forming the incline of a multi-tiered shelter. At the roof of this structure is a news clipping about the heat in Mississippi. Will it be hot in Mississippi this summer? Isn't it always?

Sometimes witnessing is an active endeavor. Mockbee and the Rural Studio plan to create

ABOVE: Aldo Rossi Arrives at Lucy's House, *2001*

OPPOSITE: The Black Warrior, *1996*

Hale County residents in front of The Children of Eutaw Pose Before Their Ancient Cabins, *1992*

twin houses for two different clients: one, poor and black; another, privileged and white. In recent, untitled drawings and paintings for these houses, Mockbee conjures the spirits of the architects Aldo Rossi and Charles Moore. Rossi, in the guise of a horse's skull balanced on a creosote-soaked wooden block and beaver sticks, visits the small cabin in which Lucy Bryant Harris now lives. In one painting, *Untitled* (2001), one of Harris's children is attended by an angel in the shadow of the cottage. The angel is a collage detail from Agnolo Gaddi's *Coronation of the Virgin* (c. 1370). Life and death, the courtly and the vernacular, the noble and the abject all come to play in the space of the painting.

The history of a moment is present in a painting even if it does not visually represent that moment. It is there in the paint itself. The subtle craters that riddle the surface of Mockbee's painting *The Black Warrior* (1996) were created when the rain fell suddenly on his open studio in Canton one summer. His own struggles with mortality are there, too, lurking in the doorways, entrances, and exits that frequently disrupt the surfaces. *The Children of Eutaw Pose Before Their Ancient Cabins* (1992) is a threshold, with recessive spaces interrupting the fiery field. Are these spaces windows or coffins? What lies on the other side of the threshold? Perhaps what lies there is a place beyond what we are asked to accept as history, a place that describes not only these families but the circumstances that have brought them, and us, to where we are at the beginning of the twenty-first century.

Mockbee has described himself as a modernist architect. His paintings, collages, and drawings also owe a debt to modernism, although it is a less obvious one. In modern art, the grid is not only a device but a myth itself. Like all myths, it is an attempt to deal with contradiction. Early creation myths describe man rising from the earth like a plant. Other, later ones, depict him as the offspring of a sexual union. Although these earlier, innocent forms of belief defy common knowledge, they are still respected. A myth allows both views to be held, because it buries those contradictions. In painting, the grid lets us think we are dealing with the "real" world, the never-ending aggression of the material sphere, and at the same time it gives us the solace of belief, the timeless quality of fiction.

In many of Mockbee's paintings, the grid is broken by shadows that call attention to these contradictions. The stories become spatialized, and the trajectory of the contradictions is unearthed. The past becomes apparent. The conflicting freedoms of de Soto's expedition and Tuscaloosa's resistance are there. So too is the tangled situation of privileged, mostly white students serving and learning from poor black folks on whose backs that privilege has been written. There is a power to Mockbee's work that is uncomfortable to many. It is frequently dismissed as an act of liberal white charity. But in his rural mythology, this act of charity is something far more dangerous. It threatens to become an act of redemption. Perhaps those who cannot be redeemed in history can be redeemed in mythology. They can find shelter from its heat in the truthful shadows of Mockbee's art.

TOP: *Walker Evans*, Bud Fields and his Family, Hale County, Alabama, *Summer 1936*

BOTTOM: *Walker Evans*, Sunday Singing, Frank Tengle's Family, Hale County, Alabama, *Summer 1936*

PHOTOGRAPHING HALE COUNTY

CERVIN ROBINSON

THOSE OF US who have never been to Hale County, home of the Rural Studio, may still know of it from photographs. We may have seen pictures taken in the summer of 1936 and published in a new edition of James Agee and Walker Evans's *Let Us Now Praise Famous Men*. We may have seen pictures by William Christenberry, a native of Alabama, in exhibitions or published in his 1983 book *William Christenberry: Southern Photographs*. Or, in architectural magazines, we may have seen pictures taken by architectural photographer Tim Hursley, whose photographs illustrate this book. We may well wonder whether the volume of this attention is a result of the momentum of Walker Evans's original accomplishment or, instead, of some local energy that was present in Agee and Evans's day, is present to this day, and may propel Samuel Mockbee's work.

A set of photographs of a place is in part a report and in part a creation; the representation is not the same as the original, and if we change the selection of photographs, we change the place created. In the original 1941 edition of *Let Us Now Praise Famous Men*, thirty-one of Walker Evans's pictures were published. In the subsequent 1960 edition, twice that number appeared. In this new edition some pictures were replacements, in at least one instance because the negative may have been lost, in other instances because Evans now preferred, to an original picture, a different one.

The substitutions result in subtle alterations; the additional photographs produce a major change in the balance of subject matter. The first edition included photographs of the three tenant families, interiors of one of their three houses, an exterior of another, two street scenes made in nearby towns, a portrait of a landowner, and an exterior of a mayor's office. The additions in the 1960 edition give far more of a sense of place, including as they do exteriors of all of the families' houses and views of fields where they worked. It also includes subjects that in 1941 were probably taken for granted (though not so much so that Evans never photographed them in the South) but that, from the changed perspective of 1960, must have seemed essential. There is a railroad station and its tracks, an abandoned antebellum plantation house, and a street scene with black men. All three subjects were presumably prevalent in Hale County in the summer of 1936, but, we learn from the 1973 Da Capo catalog *Walker Evans: Photographs for the Farm Security Administration, 1935–1938*, these three pictures had actually been taken in western Mississippi the winter before. So, though Agee's text is precisely a product of the late thirties, the photographs Evans ultimately used were very much choices of the era in which they were finally published.

William Christenberry, whose grandparents had lived "within shouting distance" of one of Agee and Evans's tenant families, came upon a copy of *Let Us Now Praise Famous Men* in 1960. The following year he began taking photographs in Hale County, eventually with the blessing of Evans, whom he came to know. His subjects are simple, run-down buildings, graves, and kudzu growths. Most of the buildings are taken head on and all of his pictures are notable for their complete absence of people. Christenberry has photographed buildings in different seasons and over spans of years; sometimes he photographs the same building repeatedly and in more or less, but not at all slavishly, the same way. A recent exhibition at the Pace Macgill Gallery in New York included a group of sixteen similar photographs

of the "Green Warehouse." He photographs a wider variety of buildings than those published by Evans, though we learn from the *Walker Evans Photographs* catalog that many similar buildings caught Evans's eye in 1936. Christenberry teaches at the Corcoran College of Art and Design in Washington and maintains a kind of distance from Alabama. R. H. Cravens writes in *Southern Photographs*, "Christenberry has admitted on occasion that he could not work year round in Alabama: 'It would be too suffocating, too overpowering. The nine hundred miles between Hale County and Washington, D.C., give me the kind of perspective I need.'"

Tim Hursley's approach to Hale County is very different from that of either Evans or Christenberry. While Evans photographed in the

ABOVE: *William Christenberry*, Kudzu with Sky (Summer), Near Akron, Alabama, *1978*

OPPOSITE: *William Christenberry*, Green Warehouse, Newbern, Alabama, *1978*

ABOVE: *Timothy Hursley*, Alberta in the Kitchen, *2001*

OPPOSITE: *Timothy Hursley*, Dead Dog in Shepard's Shack, *2001*

176

county for part of one summer, Hursley has returned repeatedly over the last eight years. And while Christenberry documents only the slowest of changes, Hursley photographs radical yearly changes, and he includes the people who are involved in those changes, both those who build a house and those who eventually live in it. Standard architectural photographs of a building when it is just finished (or perhaps almost so). These pictures show a building as its designer would like it to appear and be used, that use, if it is shown, being orchestrated for the picture. Hursley has remarkably photographed a house both before and after it has changed with use. In Hale County he has photographed buildings in a manner that would be an unreachable ideal elsewhere, one that would rarely even be imagined for the most renowned of buildings.

In the 1950s Walker Evans said that he thought a young photographer's task then was far more difficult than his had been because so much had already been photographed. William Christenberry has allayed this fear: by concentrating on some of the subjects Evans photographed in Alabama in the thirties and by "domesticating" them in a framework of slowly passing time, he achieves a quite different take on Hale County. Tim Hursley has also found fresh territory by documenting an engine of change in the county and recording its presence in multiple, positive, yearly acts.

Students and clients (with long-time Rural Studio benefactor Bob Wilson at center) discuss the Akron Boys and Girls Club

PROJECT CREDITS

BRYANT (HAY BALE) HOUSE 1994

Joseph Alcock, David Baker, Amy Batchelor, Janelle Bell, Melonie Bradshaw, Timothy Burnett, Jeff Cooper, Mark Cooper, Alison Easterwood, Todd Filbert, Christopher Fogle, Steve Hand, Scott Holmes, David Hughes, William Jernigan, Kimeran Kelley, Tae Kim, Thomas Lockhart, Tiffini Lovelace, Charles Martin, Josh Mason, David Meier, Benjamin Mosley, William Murner, John Nitz, Gustavus Orum III, Thomas Parham, William Randall III, Christopher Robinson, Raymon Rutledge, Nick Sfakianos, Christopher Smith, James Smith, Jr., Todd Stuart, Gregory Stueber, Ashley Sullivan, Jonathan Tate, Melissa Teng, James Thompson, Thomas Tretheway, Kelly Van Eaton, Timothy Vaught, Ruard Veltman, Oreon Williams

SMOKE HOUSE 1994

Scott Stafford

YANCEY CHAPEL 1995

Steven Durden, Thomas Tretheway, Ruard Veltman

CHARITY PROJECTS 1995

Audrey Courtney, Steven Hall, Brian Jernigan, Gary Owen, James Palmer, Scott Ray

WILSON HOUSE 1996

Katie Baker, Eric Bobel, Jennifer Boyles, Anna Brown, Allison Bryant, Joshua Bryant, Thomas Campbell, Kevin Carpenter, Joseph Comer, Michael Davis, Erin Elston, James Franklin, Kevin Hagerson, David Holland, Ginger Jesser, Ian Jones, Ohin Kwon, Bruce Lanier III, Andrew Ledbetter, David Lorenz, Amy McElroy, Dan Menmuir, Justin Miller, Jennifer Nelson, Elizabeth Nolen, Matthew Olive, Jennifer O'Neil, Juan Pace, Jeremy Paul, Jeffrey Pearson, Peter Phelps, Everett Pollard III, Donald Powell, Brian Purdy, Kelli Ragan, Patrick Redahan, Katherine Rees, Richael Renauld, Richard Roark, Edward Rolen, Richard Shaddix, Michael Simmons, James Smith, Jennifer Smith, Michael Spinello, Jennifer Theis, Katerine Thompson, Hollis Tidwell III, Melissa Vernie, Stephen York

AKRON PAVILION 1996

Stephen Hoffman, Todd Stuart, Jonathan Tate

HARRIS (BUTTERFLY) HOUSE 1997

William Austin, Deshannon Bogan, Dominique Boyd, Clifford Brooks, Catherine Bunn, John Cline, Jr., Elizabeth Chapman, Kristen Kepne Coleman, Joshua Daniel, Elizabeth Gagood, Jimmie Geathers, Adam Gerndt, Jobeth Gleason, Robert Hill IV, Charles Hughes, Bradley Holder, Heather Johnson, Jeffrey Johnston, Chad Jones, Melissa Kearley, John Keener, Andrew Kraeger, Jr., Michael Lackey, Jeffrey Marteski, Jeremy Moffet, Andrew Moore, Timothy Patwin, Bryan Pearson, Michael Peavy, James Pfeffer, Thomas Replogle, John Ritchie, William Ryan, Jon Schumann, Bradley Shelton, Timothy Silger, Nathan Simmons, Robert Sproull, Jr., Elizabeth Stallworth, Jimmy Turner, John Waters, Samuel Watkins, William Whittaker, Jr., Heather Wootten

HERO PLAYGROUND 1997
Joseph Alcock, Melissa Teng

SUPERSHED 1997
Jarrod Hart, Thomas Palmer, Christopher Robinson, Barnum Tiller

GOAT HOUSE 1998
Stuart Ian, Jeff Cooper

COMPOSTING PRIVY AND SHOWERS 1998
Amelia Helman, Jacquelyn Overby, Jamie Phillips

POD #1 1998
Marnie Bettridge, David Bonn, Stephen Hoffman, James Krikpatrick

EVELYN LEWIS HOUSE 1999
Rebecca Alvord, Richard Amore, Jason Andoscia, Felicia Atwell, Tori Barbrey, Matt Barrett, James Baxter, Charles Berry, Katherine Bishop, Ryan Bishop, Beverly Blalock, Jennifer Bonner, Adam Buchanan, Joe Bucher, Douglas Byrd, Brent Collins, Gabriel Comstock, Charles Cooper, Andrew Craft, Kenneth Craft III, Patricia Davenport, Trinity Davis, James Dickinson, Justin Donovan, Joseph Duncan, Jr., William Enfinger, Matt Foley, Jared Fulton, Benjamin Gambrel, Kimberly Geisler, Clark Gollotte, Jonathan Graves, Melissa Hall, Joel Hallisey, Matt Harbin, Breanna Hinderliter, Amanda Hodgins, Amy Holtz, Eric Howell, Jennifer Hughes, Emily King, Ginger Krieg, Robert Littleton, Mary Beth Maness, Elizabeth Manguso, John McCabe, Jerryn McCray, Marion McElroy, Wendy Messenger, Randall Morgan, Timothy Neal, Andrew Olds, Nathan Orrison, Derrick Owens, Laura Penn, Jennifer Pitcher, Ryan Puett, Andrea Ray, Emory Redden, Troy Redden, Ronald Renfrow, Anna Ritchie, Jennifer Rogers, Blake Rutland, Bart Rye, Jack Sanders, Jennifer Saville, Chris Shepard, Jeff Slaton, David Snyder, Jeffrey Stephens, Daniel Sweeney, Kent Thagard, Anthony Tindill, Jody Touchstone, Derek Wagner, Christopher Waters, Emmie Wayland, Jason Weyland, Joanna Wilkerson, Joe Yeager

PODS 1999
Brandi Bottwell, Andrew Ledbetter, Melissa Vernie

SEED HOUSE (MANOR BRYANT) 1999
Ian Jones, Jennifer O'Neil, Doug Shaddix

HERO CHILDREN'S CENTER 1999
Allison Bryant, Ginger Jesser, Michael Renauld, Nikol Shaw

SUPERSHED KITCHEN 1999
Melissa Vernie

PUMP HOUSE (AT MASON'S BEND) 1999
Jennifer O'Neil, Doug Shaddix

MASON'S BEND PLAZA AND BUS STOP 1999
Marcus Hurley, Scott Marek, RaSheda McCalpine, David Ranghelli, Samantha Reinhart-Taylor, Claudia Richardson, Heath Van Fleet

MASON'S BEND COMMUNITY CENTER 2000
Forrest Fulton, Adam Gerndt, Dale Rush, Jon Schumann

SPENCER HOUSE KITCHEN 2000
Jeremy Bagents, Kelly Rutledge

THOMASTON FARMER'S MARKET 2000
Jeff Johnston, Melissa Kearley, Bruce Lanier, Jimmy Turner, Jay Waters

FOREMAN TRAILER 2000
Will Brothers, Brandon Canipelli, Melissa Harold, Jennifer Hataway, Marla Holt, Lynielle Houston, Elisabeth Kelly, Bradley Martin, Ashley McClure, Meaghan Peterson, Leia Price, John Reckamp, Astyn Richard, Kevin Songer, Tracye Tidwell, Robert White

SANDERS-DUDLEY HOUSE 2001
Alicia Armbrester, Hawra Bahman, Brian Bailiff, Meredith Baker, Abby Barnett, Jason Black, Elizabeth Blaney, Lauren Bonner, Kristi Bozeman, Katie Bryan, Natalie Butts, Daniel Brickman, John Caldwell, Matt Christopher, Chris Devine, Sarah Dunn, Matthew Edwards, Elizabeth Ellington, Matthew Finley,

Briannen Foster, Azalia Golbitz, Asif Haque, Adam Hathaway, Julie Hay, Lesley Ann Hoke, Patrick Holcombe, Lynielle Houston, Jason Hunsucker, Andrew Jacobs, Kris Johnson, Charles Jorgenson, Elizabeth Kelly, Karrie Kitchens, Sophorn Kuoy, Erik Lindholm, Richard Long, Beth Lundell, Nathan Makemson, Robert Maurin, Charles Mazzola, David McClendon, Emily McGlohn, Chris McRae, Albert Mitchum, Joyce Selina Momberger, Patrick Nelson, Paul Ovnic, Michah Padgett, Brannen Park, Sheetal Patel, Leia Wynn Price, Walker Renneker, Astyn Richard, Seth Rodwell, Nia Rogers, Michael Scherer, Mike Shehi, Jennifer Sherlock, Sara Singleton, Margaret Sledge, Brandon Smith, Melissa Smith, Joel Solomon, Jen Stanton, Donna Stober, Melissa Sullivan, Laura Tarpy, Jermaine Washington, Robert White, Meghan Young

NEWBERN BASEBALL FIELD 2001

Marnie Bettridge, James Kirkpatrick, Jack Sanders

NEWBERN PLAYGROUND 2001

Nia Rogers, Margaret Sledge

AKRON PLAYGROUND 2001

Gabe Comstock, Amy Holtz, Andrew Olds

CORRUGATED BALE POD 2001

Gabe Comstock, Amy Holtz, Andrew Olds

AKRON BOYS AND GIRLS CLUB 2001

Craig Peavy, Patrick Ryan, Brad Shelton

BODARK THEATER 2001

Lee Cooper, Trinity Davis

CHANTILLY 2001

Chris Humphries

FACULTY AND STAFF

Samuel Mockbee and D. K. Ruth, co-founders

Steve Hoffman, Andrew Freear, Richard Hudgens, Christian Trask, Bryan Bell, Tinka Sack, John Forney, Jack Sanders, David Buege, Lisa Nicholson, Janet Stone, Ann Langford, Melissa Derry, Althea Huber, Melissa Gentry, Laura Smith, Nia Rodgers, Margaret Sledge, Tammie Cook, Ben Kelly, Charles Jay, Mike Thomas, Robert Steele, LeRone Smiley, Fred Brock, Donald Park, Woody Stokes, Randy Henry

BENEFACTORS

Alabama Power Foundation
John Carroll
Paul Darden
Graham Foundation for Advanced
    Studies in the Fine Arts
Interface Americas, Inc.
Jessie Ball duPont Foundation
J. F. Day and Company, Inc.
John P. and Dorothy S. Illges
    Foundation
Bruce Lanier
Bill Laver
L. E. F. Foundation
Ludwick Family Foundation
William Morrisette
Lemuel Morrison
Nathan Cummings Foundation
Jennifer O'Neil
Oprah's Angel Network
Christine Pielenz
Sharon Rhoden
Tom Rhoden
Katherine Roloson
Robert Roloson
Deedie Rose
Elizabeth Saft
Virginia Saft
Silver Tie Fund
Elizabeth Sledge
William Sledge
Jim Turnipseed
Bob Wilson
W. K. Kellogg Foundation

PATRONS

Alabama Civil Justice Foundation
Leslie Armstrong
Leland Avery
Sharon Awtry
Jeff Beard
Sue Landon Beard
Books-A-Million
Retha Brannon
Eileen Brown
James M. Brown, Jr.
Mary Ward Brown
Marka Bruhl
Charles Bunnell
California Community Foundation
Gary Citron
Geoffrey Clever
Community Foundation of Middle
    Tennessee
Theresa Costanza
Crawford McWilliams Hatcher
    Architects
Lucy Creighton
Carolyn East
Mary Edwards
Walter Fuller
Greensboro Nursing Home
Giattina Fisher & Aycock
    Architects
Tommy Goodman
Jeff Hand
Rosemary Haines
Slaughter Harrison
Everett Hatcher
Sam Hay
Garve Ivey
Mary Jolly
Kal Kardous
Jim Kellen
Russell Komesarook
Charlotte Lewter
Annemarie Marek

David Matthews
Max Protetch Gallery
Joe D. McCurry
Jerry McWilliams
Merengo County Historical
    Society
Metal Construction Association
Christina Mickel
Helen Misrachi
Scott Morgan
Beatrice Morrison
Ben Mosley
Stacy Mosley
Kate Mytron
National Trust for Historic
    Preservation
Scott Nelson
City of Newbern, Alabama
Nexus Contemporary Art Center
OPMXI
Tommy Patton
Richard Pigford
Julia Potter
Richard Rhone
William Ryan
Sahan Daywi Foundation
Serendipity Club
Bennett Shapiro
Fredricka Shapiro
Shelter State Community College
Frank Strong
Frances Sullivan
Patsy Sumrall
Kenneth Tyler
Janet Ward
Warren Ward
Wehadkee Foundation
Elizabeth Wilson
G. B. Woods
Daniel Wright
Adam Yarinsky

BIBLIOGRAPHY

Anderson, Tara. "Architecture Students Design, Build Budget Homes." *Auburn Plainsman*, 6 March 1997: section B.

Bell, Elma. "Use it Again, Sam: Architectural Students Recycle Old Materials into New Building." *Birmingham News*, 6 June 1995: pp. 1C–2C.

Blitchington, Rosemarie. "Butterflies and Hay Bales." *Wemedia* V1. January–February 2001: pp. 72–79.

Bradley, Martha Sonntag. "Mockbee Celebrates the Simple—Says Focus on People, Not Places." *Salt Lake Tribune*, 17 May 1998: p. D6.

Byars, Mel. "Tracking the Hybrid." *ARTnews*, Summer 2000: p. 26.

Culpepper, Steve. "The Art of Architecture Visits Sharecropper Country." *Fine Homebuilding* 105. November 1996: pp. 44–46.

Culver, Rhonda. "Architecture Program Builds Hope." *Auburn Plainsman*, 9 December 1993: section B.

Czarnecki, John. "Rural Studio: Samuel Mockbee's Studio at Auburn University is Rebuilding the Rural South while Educating Young Architects." *CRIT*, Spring 1997: pp. 20–24.

Dean, Andrea Oppenheimer. "The Hero of Hale County." *Architectural Record*, February 2001: pp. 76–80.

———. "Return of the Native: Photographer William Christenberry's Ongoing Portrait of his Hard Scrabble Hale County, Ala. Home." *Preservation*, May–June 1998: pp. 70–79.

Deitz, Paula. "On Design: Movers and Shapers." *ARTnews*, June 1998: p. 97.

Dietsch, Deborah. "Mockbee's Mission." *Architecture*, January 1997: pp. 49–51.

Foss, Sara. "Faith Guides Tire Chapel's Construction." *Birmingham News*, 11 November 2000: p. E5.

Fox, Catherine. "Sharing Sweat, Swinging Hammers." *Atlanta Constitution*, 21 July 1996.

Grimsley Johnson, Rheta. "A Genius Nicknamed Sambo—Grant-Winning Architect's Studio, Students Build on Lessons of Life." *Atlanta Journal-Constitution*, 22 June 2000.

Hall, Peter. "Life-Changing Buildings." *Sphere*, 1997: pp. 13–14.

Higgins, Kelly. "Rural Studio Featured in Parade." *Opelika Auburn News*. 4 April 1997: pp. A1–A2.

Houston, Caty. "Architecture Students Use 'Hands-On' Training to Help Less Fortunate." *Auburn Plainsman*, May 20, 1999: p. B2.

Hudson, Judy. "Samuel Mockbee." *Bomb Magazine*, February 2001: pp. 38–47.

Ingals, Zoe. "An Education with Hammer and Nails." *Chronicle of Higher Education* 42: 12, 15 November 1996: pp. 44–46.

Ivy, Robert. "Editorial." *Architectural Record*, May 2000: p. 23.

———. "Rural Education." *Architecture*, October 1994: pp. 62–65.

———. "Housing Innovations: American Architects are Designing More Flexible Living Spaces to Accommodate Society's Changing Priorities." *Architecture*, October 1994: p. 61.

Jodidio, Philip. "Sambo Mockbee and the Rural Studio." *Contemporary American Architects* 4, Fall 1998: pp. 122–131.

Johnson, Ken. "Art in Review; Samuel Mockbee." *New York Times*, 22 September 2000.

Koch, Aaron. "In the Eyes of the Beholder: An Interview with Sam Mockbee." *Crit* 49: p. 30.

Kochak, Jacqueline. "Auburn Professor Wins 'Genius Grant.'" *Opelika-Auburn News*, 14 June 2000: p. C1.

———. "The Sixth House of Virtue." *Opelika-Auburn News*, 9 January 2000: p. C1.

Kroloff, Reed. "Southern Comfort." *Architecture*, August 1997: pp. 90–93.

Kreyling, Christine. "The Hero of Hale County: Sam Mockbee." *Architectural Record*, February 2001: pp. 76–82.

LeBlanc, Sidney. "From Humble Sources, Earthy Elegance Springs." *New York Times*, 18 April 1996: pp. B1, B4.

Levy, Daniel. "Alabama Modern: Samuel Mockbee Creates Homes for the Poor that are Cheap, Practical—And Unconventionally Beautiful." *Time*, 1 October 2000: pp. 92–94.

Lowry, Angie. "Shelters for the Soul." *Auburn Magazine* 5: 2, Summer 1998: pp. 32–37.

Marks, Randy. "A Catalyst Beneath the Stars." *Mosaic*, Winter 2001: 6–8.

Mays, Vernon. "The Super Shed: Not Your Typical Dorm." *Architecture*, May 2000: pp. 192–199.

McCallum, Nancy. "Building With a Purpose." *Hope*, October 1997: 67–69.

McDaniel, Linda. "A Wealth of Accomplishment." *Appalachia*, January–April 2000: pp. 15–21.

Miller, Matthew. "Rural Design Studio Students Put Buildings—And Lives—Together." *Tuscaloosa News*, 10 April 1999: p. 1A.

Mockbee, Samuel with Mindy Fox. "Building Dreams: An Interview with Samuel Mockbee." *Sustainable Architecture White Papers*. Earth Pledge Foundation, 2000: pp. 207–214.

Myhrman, Matt. "Straw-Bale Karate in the Black Belt." *The Last Straw* 12, Fall 1995.

Nicholson, Lisa. "Rural Studio, Alabama: Architettura Per l'Emarginazione." *Casabella*, June 1999: pp. 38–43.

Pickett, Rhoda. "Building Homes for Needy Families Earns Acclaim for Auburn Program." *Mobile Register*, 14 June 2000: p. 1.

Plummer, William and Gail Camerson Wescott. "The Midas Touch—Rural Alabama Architect Samuel Mockbee Recycles Cast-off Materials and Lifts Up Lives." *People Magazine*, 4 December 2000: pp. 217–221.

Read, Mimi. "House Raising in the Black Belt: An Architecture Professor and his Students Build for Rural Families in Need." *House Beautiful*, June 1995: p. 70.

Ryan, Michael. "Houses From Scratch." *Parade Magazine*, 6 April 1997: pp. 14–15.

Ryker, Lori, editor. *Mockbee Coker: Thought and Process*. New York: Princeton Architectural Press, 1995.

Scott, Janny. "For 25 New MacArthur Recipients, Some Security and Time to Think." *New York Times*, 14 June 2000.

Seymour, Liz. "Samuel Mockbee: Reluctant Genius—Rural Studio cofounder receives MacArthur fellowship." *Architecture*, August 2000: pp. 27–28.

Sittenfeld, Curtis. "We Take Something Ordinary and Elevate it to Something Extraordinary." *Fast Company*, November 2000: pp. 296–308.